"Hardly a single one of my films isn't based on something that happened in my childhood."

Steven
SPIELBERG
A Retrospective

Richard Schickel
Foreword by Steven Spielberg

STERLING
New York

STERLING
New York

An Imprint of Sterling Publishing
387 Park Avenue South
New York, NY 10016

ISBN 978-1-4027-9650-0 (hardcover)
ISBN 978-1-4027-9651-7 (e-book)

Distributed in Canada by Sterling Publishing
c/o Canadian Manda Group, 165 Dufferin Street
Toronto, Ontario, Canada M6K 3H6

Created and produced by
Palazzo Editions Ltd, 2 Wood Street
Bath, BA1 2JQ, United Kingdom
www.palazzoeditions.com

Publisher: Colin Webb
Art Director: Mark Thomson
Managing Editor: Judy Barratt
Photo Editor: Steven P. Gorman

Please see picture credits on page 278 for
image copyright information

For information about custom editions, special
sales, and premium and corporate purchases,
please contact Sterling Special Sales at 800-805-5489
or specialsales@sterlingpublishing.com

Manufactured in China

10 9 8 7 6 5 4 3 2 1

Opening page: Steven Spielberg
aged around 10 and already nurturing
ambitions to be at the helm. He attended
Thomas A. Edison School in Haddonfield,
New Jersey, from 1952 to 1957—a portent,
perhaps, of his future inventiveness.

Opposite: The Museum of the Moving
Image, New York, presented a tribute
to Spielberg in 1994.

AUTHOR'S NOTE: This book is unique in one important respect—every quotation from Steven Spielberg in my narrative was given to me directly in the course of interviews I have conducted with him, beginning in 2005, when I made a documentary film about 1950s science fiction entitled *Watch the Skies*.

This means, of course, that my text reflects an obvious bias on my part: I like Steven personally and I generally approve of his work, though I have from time to time recorded criticisms of this or that individual film. Make of that what you will; I can only say that it is to me foolish —if not mean-spirited—to go to the effort of writing books or making TV shows about people you don't like and whose work you don't particularly approve of and enjoy.

For the record: We met in 1998 when *Time* magazine, for which I then worked part time as a movie reviewer, asked me to make a little film for a 75th anniversary party they were presenting at Radio City Music Hall. Along with several others, Spielberg had been asked to speak about, and show a short film about, a historically important American figure. He had chosen John Ford as his subject, and I helped him to make that film. We got along very nicely. I found him to be an unpretentious and genial figure and, most important, my kind of guy. By which I mean that I had his full and undivided attention when we were working on this very agreeable little project. It was not something he did by remote control.

Subsequently, we stayed in casual—occasionally not-so-casual—contact. He was, for example, executive producer on a film of mine called *Shooting War*, about World War II combat cameramen. He was, I thought, an ideal executive producer. When viewing rough cuts he said very little, but what he said was spot on. He would always home in on the weak or questionable aspects of the film, without making you feel foolish for not noticing what you had omitted or done wrong.

Later I made a film about him, which resulted in the longest of the interviews I have drawn upon here. There were also other occasions when I interviewed him. There was another of my television programs, a long *Time* article about *Munich*, and, of course, there have been interviews specifically for this book. I do not want to pretend that we are intimate friends. I will say that we are always glad to see one another, that we speak comfortably when one or the other of us has a question we need to resolve.

As to this book—it focuses on Spielberg's career as a film director. I do not detail his work as a producer— he has produced or executive-produced more than 160 films. This includes many of his own movies, of course, as well as feature films by other directors, TV programs and series, documentaries, animated films—really just about everything under the sun. In fact, he allocates more time to such efforts than any other director in the movies and his work as a producer is fully listed in the filmography. Nor have I gone into any detail about his executive responsibilities as a founder, along with Jeffrey Katzenberg and David Geffen, of DreamWorks SMG Studios. It was set up in 1994 and subsequently sold to Paramount in 2005. Probably for Spielberg the most important aspect of this venture proved to be his mentoring of younger filmmakers through the early stages of their careers. Significantly there was a gap of almost four years (1993 to 1997), with the distractions of DreamWorks getting up and running, when Spielberg made no films of his own.

Also this book has very little to say about Spielberg's life away from his work, about which I know next to nothing. This is as it should be, I think. He is a private man and he is entitled to his privacy, particularly since there are plenty of fascinating issues to discuss when it comes to the professional choices he has made over the years.

It should be obvious that some of what Spielberg said to me found its way into the films and articles that resulted from these interviews, but surprisingly little. I'd guess that perhaps no more than 10 or 15 percent of it made the final cuts and edits of the work—which does not mean that the rest of it is dross. It's just that you run out of time and space when you're shaping the final product. It also does not mean that he has not said something similar to other interviewers on some of the topics we take up herein. There is, however, a tone here that I think is unique—a willingness to diverge from the subject at hand, for instance, a willingness to speak anecdotally that I don't find very regularly in other sources. He does not give very many interviews—at least compared to most other directors—and he tends to stick narrowly to the point of the occasion.

No deep secrets are revealed here. As a matter of fact, I don't think Spielberg has much of a dark side. He is too busy for that indulgence. This is, then, a short working portrait of a man I find likable and whose work— particularly in its range and technical finesse—I find astonishing and rewarding and in important respects still undervalued. He is really too fecund for his own good, which is not to say that he lacks for wealth, prizes, and the general high regard of moviegoing mankind.

In any case, I am pleased to call him my friend, and to offer this book as a token of that friendship.

RICHARD SCHICKEL

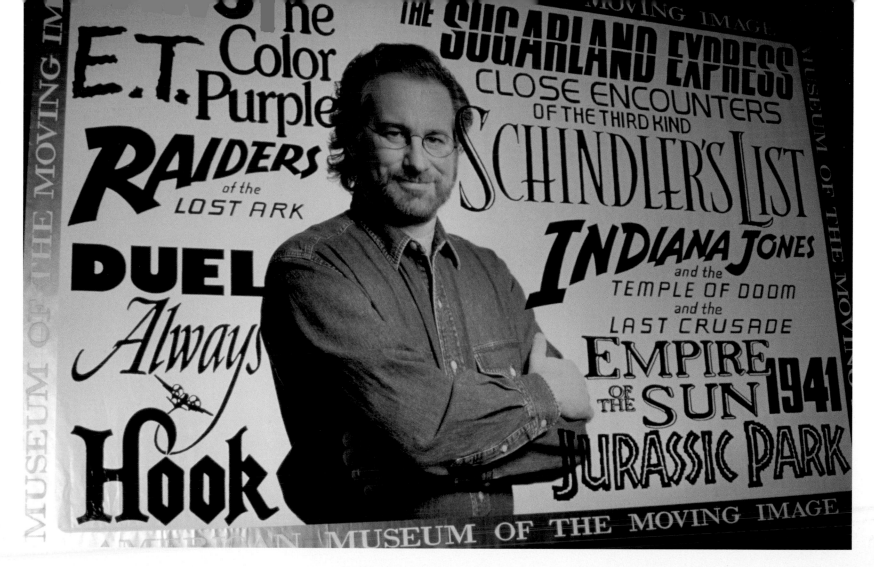

Contents

Foreword

There are a couple of things this book is not. It is not a full-scale biography or a disguised autobiography. It does, however, consist of excerpts from a number of interviews Richard Schickel has conducted with me over the years since we first met. In them, I have commented on the movies I've made in a career that began with some television shows I directed beginning in 1969 at Universal.

I have been fortunate to have had commercial success and a certain amount of critical favor. I have made movies that I've been proud of; and those that turned out to be less than I meant them to be did not sidetrack me for long. More important—far more important—I have had an extraordinarily happy life. I have done the things I love best to do—directing movies (28 of them over the course of four decades) and, above all, have enjoyed the blessings of a loving family life.

Family is not a matter that greatly concerns this book. My conversations with Richard have centered around the films I have made (and some that, for one reason or another, I decided not to make), and that's as it should be, I think. Richard agrees that what someone of public prominence owes to his audience is an accounting of those activities—in my case movies—that he offers to them for their approval. They may, or may not, be interested in why certain choices were made over the course of my career, which is now starting to surprise me with its longevity. I am not ruling out the possibility of someday writing some sort of memoir about my life, but I don't think that I'll be doing that in the very near future. I love making movies, whether I'm directing them myself or producing the works of younger directors with pictures that interest me—and I think will interest a larger audience. I can honestly say that I am as enthusiastically committed to film today as I was all those years ago when I first began making my amateur pictures when I was in high school.

In fact, my commitment has probably grown, as my techniques and ambitions have inevitably expanded. I still like to make movies of the *Indiana Jones* and *Jurassic Park* variety. They present more challenges to me as a director than may seem obvious to some people. They're fun to make and, apparently, fun for audiences to see. But there's no doubt in my mind

In profile while on location for *Close Encounters of the Third Kind*, 1977.

that, from the time of *The Color Purple*, I've been increasingly drawn to darker material. As you grow older, you just naturally want to turn to stories that take up more serious subjects than, say, big sharks and even bigger dinosaurs.

This does not mean that I disown any of my films, even the ones I now realize that I might have done better. We can sometimes, maybe perversely, love our failures as much as we do our successes—if only because we can learn more from them than we do from our hits.

That, however, leaves out of the conversation the matter of luck, of which I have had a good share. It begins with the mentors I was fortunate to acquire very early in my career. I cannot say enough about men like Sid Sheinberg, Lew Wasserman, and Richard Zanuck, who saw something in me that I didn't fully see in myself. I was lucky, too, in that I did not have to undergo a long apprenticeship. I was making television shows at Universal when I was in my early twenties and I directed *Duel*, a made-for-TV film that was later released here and there as a feature, when I was 24. Four years later, when *Jaws* was bedeviled by all the difficult conditions that shooting on water imposes— not to mention a mechanical shark that refused to behave—it was Sid who stood by me when almost everyone else wanted to shut down the production or, at the very least, fire the director. The first time Sid and I talked about my working at Universal he had said he would stand by me in good times and bad, and he was true to his words. The picture was finished—belatedly—and it was a success. I will always have ambivalent feelings about it, because it was such hard and scary work. But there is no question in my mind that it was Sid's grace under pressure that permitted me to continue my life as a director when the issue was very much in doubt.

So, yes, luck. And the instinct to avoid certain pitfalls and to embrace certain opportunities. And enough knowledge to realize acceptably most of the jobs I took on—understanding that disappointments are inevitable and not to be whined about.

I hope this book turns out to be part of my good luck. I have never, in the past, cooperated with books about me. But the author is a friend and occasional colleague, and we seem to talk easily and he makes no pretense of being definitive—and I respect his judgment. Within his narration he has simply recorded a number of my thoughts about the work I have been pursuing for so long. There are more, but I think these are enough for the interested reader to get an idea of how I try to approach my work, and the pleasure I unfailingly derive from it. Although normal retirement age is around the corner, I want to go on working forever as, apart from anything else, directing movies is both my purest passion and my greatest pleasure.

Steven Spielberg

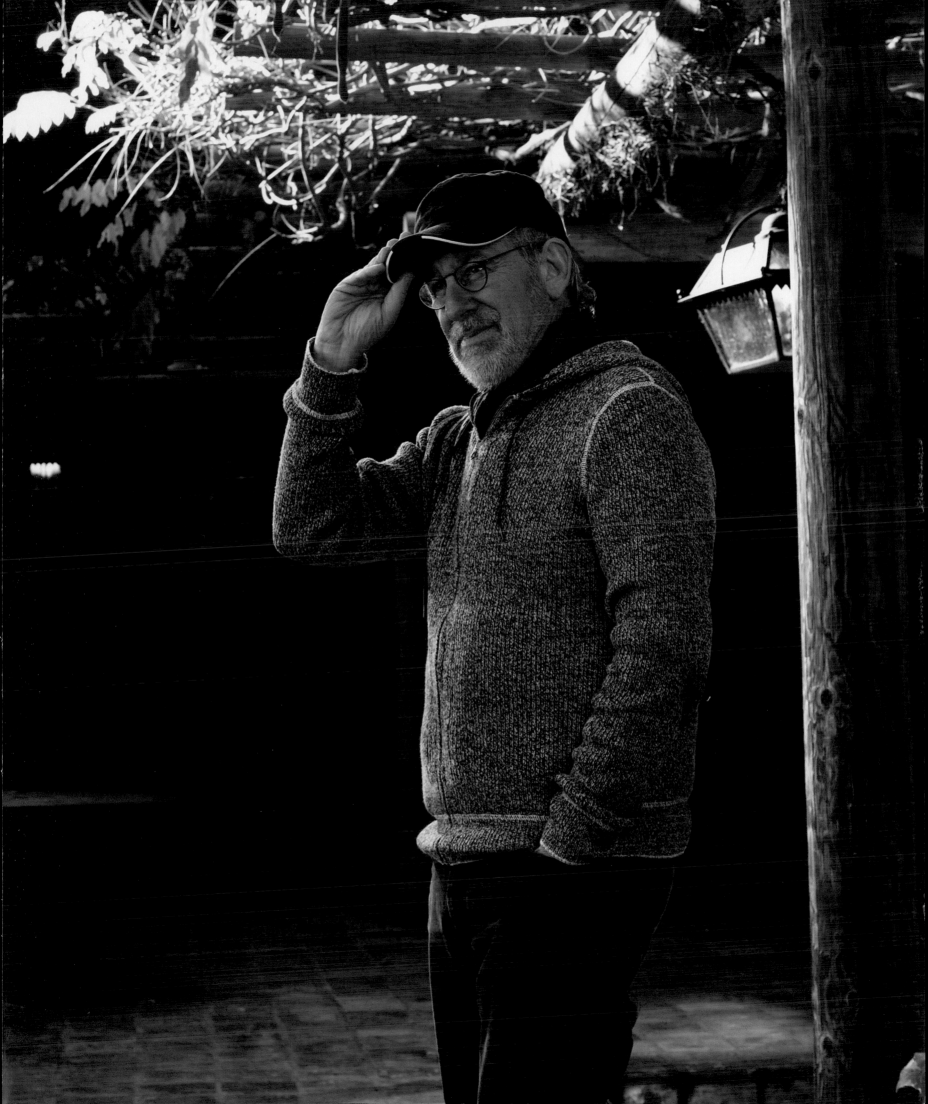

"When I realized I could make life better for me, through this medium, this little 8mm rinky dink medium, I felt really good about my life, myself and, you know, possibly bringing some other people into this amazing medium."

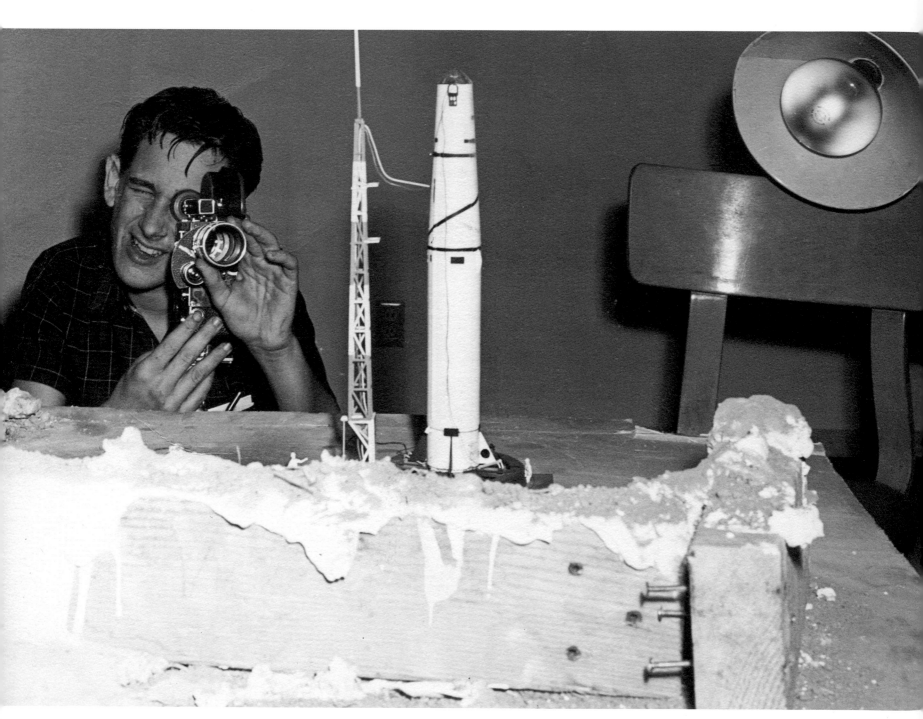

Aged 17, and preparing for lift-off on the *Firelight* set.

The Beginner

One day, when he was about 18 years old, spending his summer vacation with relatives in Canoga Park, Steven Spielberg decided to take the Universal Studios tour. In those days the tours were made by buses and, midway, there was a bathroom break, which the young would-be filmmaker took. The difference between him and his fellow tourists was that when they clambered back on the bus, he stayed behind, hiding in one of the stalls. After they departed, he emerged a half hour later, free to wander the lot unhampered.

Was this an impulsive gesture? Or was it a carefully planned escape to his future? One has to believe it was the latter. As his subsequent career demonstrates, Steven Spielberg is not a notably impulsive man; many of his most important films have gestated for a decade and more. But essentially it doesn't matter. "I was on the Universal Studios lot. I had no idea how I'd get home, but I spent the whole afternoon just walking in and out of doors—sound stages, cutting room—and took my own tour and had an amazing time."

Eventually, however, quitting time approached, and Steven had no idea of how to get back to Canoga Park. It was time to make a phone call. Fortuitously, he approached a man named Chuck Silvers, head of the film library, who heard his story, laughed appreciatively at it, praising his chutzpa, and most important, wrote him out a three-day pass, which the kid put to excellent use. At the end of that period, however, he was on his own. He decided to see if he could get by on sheer nerve. Dressing himself in his best Bar Mitzvah suit—people in those days still wore their best clothes to work in the studios—waving his out-of-date pass at Scotty, the always smiling main-gate guard—he simply strolled on the lot and continued to do so, unchallenged, for the rest of the summer. And for the following summer, too.

He was never once stopped. There are always people bustling about at the studios intent on errands that no one ever questions. The trick is to look intent. And to never look back. In a relatively short time, people just assumed that Spielberg had some kind of job at the studio, though no one ever inquired what, exactly, that might be.

"I've had a story for a long time about my mom and dad that I'm too chicken to make. I'm going to make it some day. But it's hard because I'm taking some deeply personal events of my mom, dad, three sisters, and my life and putting it up there for the whole world to see. I have to go to Oz to ask the wizard for some courage before I make that movie."

Spielberg didn't know either. "I never had a big thought about what I could do with movies in those days," he recalls. Is that possible? I think it is. Certainly it is more likely than the thought that he was embracing the "discovery myth," the notion—retailed in dozens of books, plays, and movies—of a naïve youngster who does something more or less accidentally remarkable, breaches the walls of the studio and achieves stardom.

Spielberg, in any case, was best known in the humbler regions of the studio—where the editors, sound editors, and music mixers toiled—and one day the chief editor, Richard Belding, asked him if he wanted to make himself useful. Of course he did. Fine, go down to room 205 (or some such) and fetch a Moviola. Just tell the occupant that the machine was needed elsewhere. In the lad marched, confronting a massive, sweating, naked-to-the-waist individual, unplugged the editing machine and started wheeling it out. Screams, perhaps a brief inconsequential struggle, ensued, before the kid beat a hasty retreat—to a band of guffawing below-the-line workers. He had not recognized the outraged man at the Moviola as Marlon Brando, working on some 16mm footage taken at his Tahitian retreat and ensconced in an editing room during his tenure on a Universal contract. Spielberg, incidentally, never saw him again, though they once had a brief phone call many years later.

Essentially—and however tenuously—Spielberg was an insider looking out in those days. Which is much better than being in the opposite situation. More important, he was learning how to conduct himself in a (semi)professional way—studying the lingo, learning, for better or worse, how a studio operated, how its routines benefited efficiency—

The Spielberg family, circa 1951. From left to right: sister Anne, father Arnold, Steven, and mother Leah. Arnold and Leah were to have two more daughters, Sue and Nancy. They would divorce in the mid-1960s.

Opposite and overleaf: Photos from the family album. Many childhood memories and experiences would significantly influence Spielberg's future films.

"I kind of rebelled against the piano music because it was something that I just didn't understand. My mom played classical music and, to a child especially, that was horrid—that was the sounds of the violins in *Psycho* just striking the fingernails against the blackboard—and I used to scream bloody murder, my mom could not console me."

and sometimes threatened creativity. He has never been a rebel against authority—for the longest time, indeed, he has been one of Hollywood's chief authorities. Finally, two things: He developed an unwavering affection for Universal—his offices are still on the lot—and whatever doubts he had about his career path were settled by the time his informal relationship with the studio came to an end. He would be a director.

But then, he always had been, whether he admitted it or not. For he had long since tasted the power implicit in that position.

HE SAW HIS FIRST MOVIE when he was five years old—Cecil B. DeMille's *The Greatest Show on Earth*, which his father took him to see in Cincinnati. And it was pretty much love at first sight; he became a movie fan almost immediately, soon enough slipping the bonds of parental control. By the time he was 12 or 13 he had commandeered his father's 8mm Kodak movie camera and was making his own movies, which were by no means modest. One of them, *Firelight*, was two and a half hours long. Shot silent (but with a sound track later added), it required a year to complete. Spielberg has said that it is one of the four worst movies ever made, but, really, considering the age and inexperience of its writer-director, it is not all that bad. And he arranged a premiere of it at a local theater, complete with limousines.

The Spielbergs were, in those days, a peripatetic family. They lived in a half-dozen American cities as his father, Arnold, a computer engineer, sought ever-better jobs (his mother, Leah, was a pianist and, latterly, the proprietor of a delicatessen on Los Angeles' Pico Boulevard).

Steven was perpetually the new kid in class and never happy in that role. His was also a fractious family; Steven loved them all (he had three sisters, all younger than him) but, eventually, the parents divorced, which was traumatic for Spielberg—he has described learning to live without his father's presence in the house as the most difficult passage of his young years.

The issue for him was control—or rather the lack of it. As it is for most kids. They have to do what their parents are bound to do—change cities, homes, schools, for reasons that make sense only in the abstract. He recalls being friendless in his several schools, for example, then finally making friends, and then being forced abruptly to move on. He recalls, too, mild but palpable anti-Semitism. There was only one place he was really happy; that was in his filmmaking:

"I was infatuated with the control that movies gave me, in creating a sequence of events—a train wreck with two Lionel trains that I could then repeat and see over and over again. I think it was just a realization that I could change the way I perceived life through another medium, to make it come out better for me." And, incidentally, "to see if what I was making was having an effect on anybody other than myself."

What Spielberg was not infatuated with was college. While he was "infiltrating" Universal, he enrolled at Long Beach's California State College (it appears that his grades were not good enough to gain him admission to one of the better film schools—USC, UCLA—which were the obvious places for him to be). He was, for want of something better to do, an English major, even though he was then not a great reader. The college did not, at the time, offer a single film course, which did not deter him. He scrounged up funding

"I think all children experience filmmaking. When their parents buy them a birthday present of little characters, soldiers, little men —when I was a kid it was cowboys—and the kid lies down on the shag rug on his stomach, holds the little figure up right by his eyes so it's very realistic, and gets an angle on that soldier, puts the other soldier at arm's length in the other hand, and goes, *bang, bang, bang, bang!*—that's the beginning of filmmaking. We all start out as filmmakers. And I guess I never grew out of it."

The director of *Firelight* commandeers his father's 8mm movie camera.

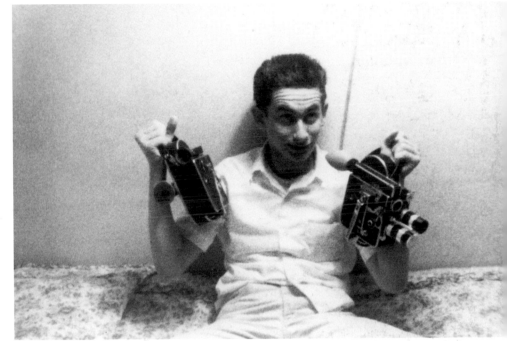

15

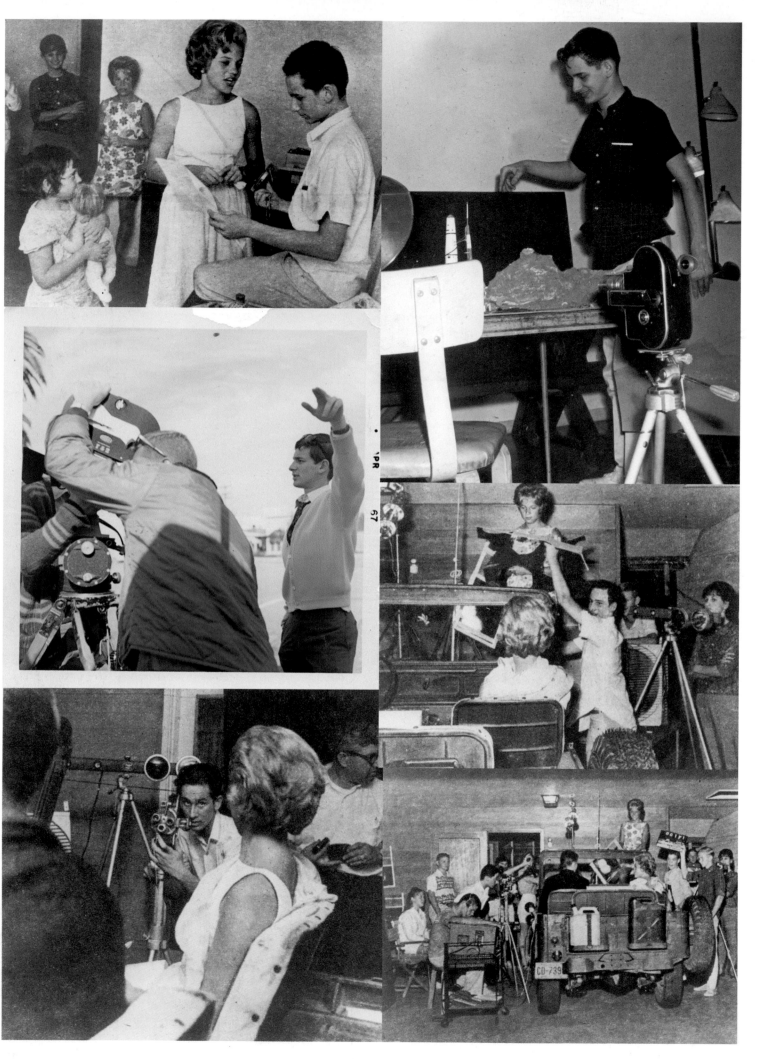

In the thick of his first effort, *Firelight*, a movie that was two and a half hours long and took a year to make. The local newspaper referred to Spielberg as "The Teenage Cecil B."

to make something like a half-dozen short films in his spare time, though perhaps it is more appropriate to see higher education as his part-time work.

Among the films he made in this period were *Encounter*, about a hit man who does not have a gun and has to make do at his trade with a knife, and, perhaps more promisingly, *Slipstream*, a bicycle-chase movie set in Palos Verdes, which he got Tony Bill to star in. Alas, he ran out of money before that film was completed. By this time, he saw "no useful purpose" in college, but the Vietnam War was on, and he needed his student deferment—it was "a capital investment in my life," as he puts it now.

He arranged his college schedule so that he took all his courses on Monday and Tuesday, leaving himself free to report for his non-job at Universal the remaining three days of the week. Most important, he realized that, promising as some of the films he had made up to this point were, he had to make something of wide general appeal, something that would make studio executives take notice of him.

Enter *Amblin'*. It existed, at first, as a five-page concept—the story of two teenage would-be lovers, flirting with one another against the bleak background of the Mojave Desert.

He showed this document to a man named Denis Hoffman, owner of a special effects house called Cinefex, but eager to become a producer. He put up $10,000, enough to make the 26-minute film, which, like *Firelight*, had no dialogue—that would come later—but did have sound effects. Spielberg has said that it seemed little more than a "Pepsi commercial," but it is something more than that—if only because it is very professionally made. Hoffman took it around to a few film festivals where it won some prizes, and later placed it at Paramount, to serve as a curtain-raiser in some locales for the mighty 1970 hit *Love Story*.

In the meantime, Spielberg had forged a relationship with a colorful and effective mentor, named Jennings Lang, who was head of production at Universal. He was a great rough-hewn character, known for mixing devastating martinis and for allegedly having one of his testicles shot off by the producer Walter Wanger, who suspected him—correctly—of trifling with his wife, the actress Joan Bennett. He took a shine to Spielberg and found his early films promising, though he did not offer him employment at the studio. He was more a wise man, a guide, if you will, to the ins and outs of studio politics.

Above: In making *Firelight*, Spielberg became immersed in the commercial as well as the creative side of the movie business. He organized a premiere on March 24, 1964, which he calculated made him a profit of one dollar on the film's $500 budget.

"It was going to be a tone poem about a boy and a girl who meet in the desert hitch-hiking their way to the Pacific Ocean. Very simple story, I wrote it in a day."

24 minutes 16 mm color
of "where it's at" today

Starring Pamela McMyler and Richard Levin

Amblin

"It took 20 minutes to write, 10 days to shoot, and six weeks to cut. It takes no position on marijuana and sex . . . just simply presents them."
—The Los Angeles Times

• Nominee, 1970 Academy Awards
• Winner, Silver Phoenix Trophy 1969 Atlanta Film Festival "World's Best Short Subject
• Winner, C.I.N.E. Golden Eagle Award

Produced by
Denis C. Hoffman
Written, directed and edited by
Steven Spielberg

Distributed by

U P A

United Productions of America
Burbank, Calif.
Sales Office:
600 Madison Avenue
New York, N.Y. 10022
Phone: 212 752-1464

It was the promise he showed on *Amblin'*—his last film as an amateur—that secured Spielberg's contract with Universal. In recognition of the movie's significance, he later named his production company after it.

It was Chuck Silvers, Spielberg's first mentor at the studio, who apparently got *Amblin'* to Sid Sheinberg, then in charge of television production at the studio. A decisive man, who would become Spielberg's most significant godfather at Universal as he himself rose to be in charge of production there, he one day summoned Spielberg to an 11 o'clock meeting in his office. "I was there at 10:40 the next morning—embarrassingly early—and had to wait about 15 minutes. When Sid saw me that was the moment he offered me a seven-year contract—within 10 minutes of meeting me."

In Sheinberg's recollection, Spielberg turned white as a ghost at this turn of events, and hesitated briefly before responding, causing the executive to wonder if perhaps he was entertaining an offer from some other studio. That was not the case; he was simply "poleaxed." At which point, Sheinberg said the magic words: "If you join us here at Universal I can guarantee you one thing: I will support you in success, but I will also support you in failure."

"That sentence," says Spielberg, "I've never forgotten."

He, naturally, signed on.

A few days later, sitting in his little office, awaiting his first assignment, he felt as if "Universal Studios had always been my home, more familiar to me than the house I grew up in. That's a horrible, heinous thing to say. I love my mom and my dad and my sisters. But this is where I belonged."

This, of course, proved to be the case. To this day, even though he has made pictures at virtually every studio in town, his production company is headquartered near the Universal backlot in a not particularly imposing, but very comfortable, adobe building, which he shows no sign of ever abandoning. The walls are adorned with Norman Rockwell paintings from his collection, as well as, in a glass case, one of the sleds from *Citizen Kane*. In the conference room there is a scale model of his latest toy, *Seven Seas*, an ocean-going yacht.

In 1969 such acquisitions were, naturally, far from his thoughts, as he contemplated his first Universal assignment, the pilot segment for Rod Serling's *Night Gallery*, which was to star no less than Joan Crawford. His was to be the centerpiece of this enterprise, with the flanking stories directed by Boris Sagal and Barry Shear.

Spielberg studies Pamela McMyler, one of the would-be lovers in *Amblin'*. Spielberg thought it little more than a "Pepsi commercial."

To hear Spielberg tell it, his career was almost over before it even began.

The picture had Crawford, as a blind woman, buy a poor man's eyes so that she could see New York before darkness fell completely. She witnesses, instead, a blackout and the riotous consequences thereof. It was a pretty ambitious project for a first-time director, not made any easier by the fact that his crew was vast—some 75 people, as opposed to the handful he was used to on his amateur shoots. Moreover, they were Hollywood veterans, who had made some of Spielberg's "favorite pictures of all time," producing "the Golden Age of Hollywood."

The result, on the first days of shooting, was predictable: "When I showed up with my acne and my long hair and the viewfinder pretentiously around my neck, like some kind of talisman that would protect me from evil, they took one look at me and said, this kid better prove himself quickly or he's out of here.

"I remember being greeted by tremendous hostility from the crew, almost like I posed some sort of threat to their security. The rank and file of the crew were just sending daggers my way, working as slowly as they could, not to get themselves fired, but maybe to get me pushed off the show. I wound up four days behind on my first professional job.

"Predictably, the studio was yelling at me and the producer, William Sackheim, was yelling at me and [future director] John Badham, the associate producer [and Spielberg friend], was saying, 'Can't you catch up a little bit?'

"It was brutal—a real baptism of fire. Whether they did it maliciously, or because I was, you know, the pledge in this fraternity and we're the active members and we're going to put you through hell week, I don't know. But it was hell week."

What saved him were the people he was working most closely with—the cameraman, Dick Bachelor, and his actors, including Joan Crawford herself and Barry Sullivan and Tom Bosley. They were all veteran professionals, of course, and the people the public wanted to see. They had no choice but to help the kid through his ordeal.

The results, naturally, turned out to be mixed. The show premiered on NBC, received good ratings and turned into a series. Nevertheless, Spielberg heard himself referred to around the lot as "Sheinberg's folly." He hung around for what seemed to him an eternity, getting very little work—he did a *Marcus Welby, MD* a few months later, but did not return to steady employment thereafter for over a year. His most notable work was probably the *Columbo* episode that was not the pilot, but rather the first episode in the history of that long-running series. In the interim between *Welby* and his return to the studio, he requested, and received from Sheinberg, a leave of absence (he simply tacked the missing months on to the end of his contract) and worked on some speculative scripts, with results that turned out to be more than a little promising.

One such item was the idea that eventually turned into his first feature, *The Sugarland Express*. It was based on the true story of a slightly addled couple (eventually played by Goldie Hawn and William Atherton), who attempt to rescue their child from foster-parenthood, and in the process become folk heroes in Texas, where the film, essentially one long chase, is set. Universal had acquired some public-domain material on the story, Spielberg got wind of it, co-wrote a treatment of it, and turned it over to his friends Hal Barwood and Matthew Robbins, who received writing credits on the film. They were part of a group of young filmmakers (Martin Scorsese, George Lucas and Brian De Palma, among others) who were clinging to the lower levels of the industry, making, or trying to make, their first low-budget films, meantime reading each other's scripts, helping solve one another's problems and even doing their best to preserve films, which, in those days before home video, the studios were uninterested in doing.

With Barwood and Robbins hard at work, Spielberg turned to another idea, a script he had written with a college friend, Claudia Salter. It was called *Ace Eli and Rodger of the Skies*. It told the story of a World War I flying ace barnstorming in early 1920s America, accompanied by his wise-child son. Aviation is a theme that recurs often in Spielberg's later films, as does that of troubled relationships between parents and children.

The script attracted the attention of Richard Zanuck and David Brown, then at the beginning of their long partnership as independent producers. They offered Spielberg and Salter $100,000 for it—by far the most money Spielberg had ever seen in his brief movie career. They, of course, grabbed it and the picture was set up at Twentieth Century-Fox, with Cliff Robertson in the starring role. There may have been some talk of Spielberg directing the project, but after working with Robertson on a production rewrite, the picture passed from his hands—Salter received sole writing credit, with Spielberg getting story credit, and John Erman directed. The once promising film eventually received a very limited release and was a notable flop, critically and commercially.

Spielberg, however, was undaunted. He was a relentless networker in those days—not only with the young would-be directors of his own age, but also with highly placed executives at Universal and elsewhere. Whatever setbacks he endured, people from Sheinberg on down continued to believe in his talent. He was a demonic worker and, though somewhat shy and reserved around people he did not know, he was good-natured and loyal to his friends and mentors. Many of these relationships were to become lifelong.

"Sheinberg's folly" here with his mentor Sid Sheinberg (left) watching video playback of *Always*, 1989.

In 1970–71 he was back at Universal. And was working steadily. In those years he made a half-dozen TV episodes, the most notable of which was the *Columbo* episode. The series joined NBC's regular schedule in September of 1971. In some ways Spielberg's contribution to it was a minor classic, with all of Peter Falk's tics and tricks very much in eccentric place, but not yet the clichés they would eventually become.

But Spielberg's career was still merely promising—especially given his youth (he was 24 in 1971). No one doubted that he was going to enjoy a major directorial career in the movies. On the other hand, no one was predicting, at this point, the power, the wealth, the acclaim that was to accrue to him in a matter of just four years—especially since the first instrument of his transformation was, all things considered, such a modest project.

"Every time I find something new, it's always about a story. Whenever I find something new to do, I get excited again. I become a kid again. The fountain of youth for me is an idea or a story. I either come up with it myself or read something that somebody else writes and I say, 'Oh my God, I've got to tell that story. I've got to make that movie.' That's what keeps me going."

Preparing a shot for *Jaws* under testing conditions.

Overleaf: Surveying the Dog Green section of Omaha Beach from a German gun position while filming the unforgettable 25-minute combat sequence that opens *Saving Private Ryan* (1998). This was the second film for which Spielberg won an Oscar for best director, the first being *Schindler's List* (1993).

The Director

"If a movie is going to be a reflection of any kind of a real-life situation, it has to have all the sine waves of real stories, meaning there's absurdity, there's comedy, there's tragic loss, there's huge impenetrable forces chasing you down, and then there's redemption at the end."

DUEL

(1971)

"*Duel* is an indictment of machines. And I determined very early on that everything about the film would be the complete disruption of our whole technological society."

"When we released the film theatrically, the Europeans saw it for the first time in one aspect ratio of 1.85:1, and on TV I didn't even see this because the sides were cut off, but in 1.85:1 I'm in 17 shots in the back seat of the car, fully revealed. They had to optically blow it up and go in and reposition to get me out of there."

On the face of it, *Duel* was a trim little film—suspenseful, full of action, and, most interesting, touched with a kind of motiveless malignity. For reasons never adequately explained, the driver of a huge, battered truck decides to stalk and try to kill a more or less innocent motorist—a salesman making a routine out-of-town call—on a largely deserted stretch of desert highway. OK, the driver of the car (Dennis Weaver) had accidentally cut the truck off in the first reel, but, really, it is not an event that calls for murderous revenge—maybe some pushing and shoving should they happen to encounter one another at a rest stop along the way.

On the road to big-screen success. *Duel* started out as a TV movie in 1971, but an extended theatrical version was released in Europe two years later.

Previous page: On a sparse notice board in his first office, Spielberg displays early acclaim for *Duel* from the Taormina Film Festival in Sicily.

Dennis Weaver checks
his rearview mirror.
Each stage of the journey
would only get worse.

The studio had acquired Richard Matheson's *Playboy* story more or less routinely, thinking it might do as a modestly budgeted feature or, more likely, a movie of the week on television. It was Spielberg's assistant at the time, Nona Tyson, who read it and brought it to Spielberg's attention. "You should direct this," he recalls her saying. "This is you. This is up your alley." "How she knew this, I don't know," Spielberg says, but after one reading of the script, which Matheson had written, he became "infatuated" with the property. He went to the producer George Eckstein, his *Columbo* reel in hand, and began campaigning for the picture.

Whereupon, he caught a lucky break. For some reason someone at the studio thought *Duel* might be a Gregory Peck feature, which would have changed the whole equation of the enterprise; it almost certainly would have entailed assigning a more "important" director to it. Worse, it would have changed the whole tenor of the film. Peck was a heroic actor. You could not imagine him deeply menaced, let alone panicked by the film's central situation. Dennis Weaver was quite another matter. He had played Chester, the gimpy deputy, on TV's *Gunsmoke* for many years—an everyman if ever there was one. Him you could imagine being scared out of his wits by this situation—and somehow drawing on reserves, if not of bravery, then of cunning, as he fights his way out of it. In any case, Peck passed on the film, and Weaver got the part.

Spielberg recalls: "The way I saw it, it was a 'big bully' story. Not only was the truck a bully, but everyone on the highway was a bully—everybody at the gas stations, the laundromat, the café. His wife was a bully; the woman who came in to do the laundry was a bully. The waitress was the only nice person in the entire movie. It was a very bad week for this man; he was going to have to find a way to survive

Posters for the film's big-screen release in Japan (left), Poland (top, right), and France (bottom, right) in 1973. Did Jan Mlodozeniec, the designer of the shark-like graphic on the Polish poster, know something Spielberg didn't?

Weaver squares up to his faceless adversary on a highway somewhere in the Mojave Desert.

the worst week of his entire life. That was my attitude going into the show. That was the tone I tried to set."

The incidents of the story are relatively mild. It takes a while for Weaver's character (David Mann) to realize that the truck is actually stalking him and perhaps it's only an incident when the truck lays waste a roadside attraction— a snake farm, with the poisonous creatures getting loose and menacing—that is truly spectacular. It may be, though, that the scariest scene of all takes place in a diner, where Weaver looks up and realizes that among the big rig drivers waiting for their chow, one of them must be his nemesis.

Spielberg says he was falsely credited with turning *Duel* into a Hitchcockian story. He gives most of the credit to Matheson's sparsely dialogued script—"very Hitchcocky and suspenseful." He adds: "I think that was the first time I realized, 'Hey, if I have a good script and I'm a good director, I can make a pretty terrific movie,' the first time I really embraced the idea that directors need great screenplays to look good."

Which is not to diminish Spielberg's role in the film. This was a TV movie—an 11-day schedule, a 74-minute

running time, "kind of like a feature," as Spielberg says. But not quite, in that it was shy of minimum feature length by at least 15 minutes. Even so, it would require carefully detailed planning, which, as it turned out, Spielberg was more than up for.

He didn't storyboard the picture. Instead, he drew a map of the stretch of highway in the Mojave Desert where he would be working. On this he drew little Vs, indicating where he would place his cameras (at some points in the chase sequences he had as many as five of them operating simultaneously), "so within one mile of highway I could get a whole lot of shots—at least five angles—then turn the vehicles around, change lenses and then go the other way, going not only from right to left, but from left to right as well." He was helped, too, because Matheson had laid out the story on paper "visually and quite wonderfully."

Spielberg finished on time. And the studio received the picture ecstatically. It was broadcast on NBC on November 13, 1971, and received good ratings and better reviews. There was, at the time, a lot of press interest in the movie of the week, a feeling that this longish format carried the

possibility of breaking out of the routines of episodic television, and this modest, but expert little film fulfilled that promise.

That was because it was more than just, well, a duel. It tapped into a very common anxiety. You're going along, minding your own business, make a common, basically forgivable mistake, and find yourself, all of a sudden, for no particular rhyme or reason, fighting for your life—in this case on an anonymous highway, where, essentially, no one cares whether you live or die. You could regard it as a smart, suspenseful, rather basic thriller. Or you could respond to its existential implications.

There were enough of those that the studio decided to release a somewhat expanded theatrical version of the film in Europe two years later, where it won some film festival prizes, and even engendered some goofy controversy. Was it, perhaps, a study in class warfare? The blue-collar truck driver seeking revenge on the middle-class salesman, blithely unaware of the Marxist implications of the story?

Spielberg had no comment on that, but the story was not quite finished. A decade later, when Spielberg was a much more famous director, yet another version of *Duel* was tentatively released in a few American markets, where it did not prosper—and no matter. For the moment, he was just glad finally to have begun to fulfill the promise everyone had seen in him, to have the freedom to move forward on his first official theatrical film. He would later reflect that *Duel* did have a profound influence on the film that made him a superstar director. But *Jaws* was, at that point, not even a dream, except perhaps in the imagining mind of the novelist Peter Benchley. Spielberg's preoccupation, for the moment, was his upcoming first official theatrical movie—*The Sugarland Express*.

TI

DUE

Starring
DENNIS WEAVER Screenp
Directed by STEVEN SPIELBERG · Produced b

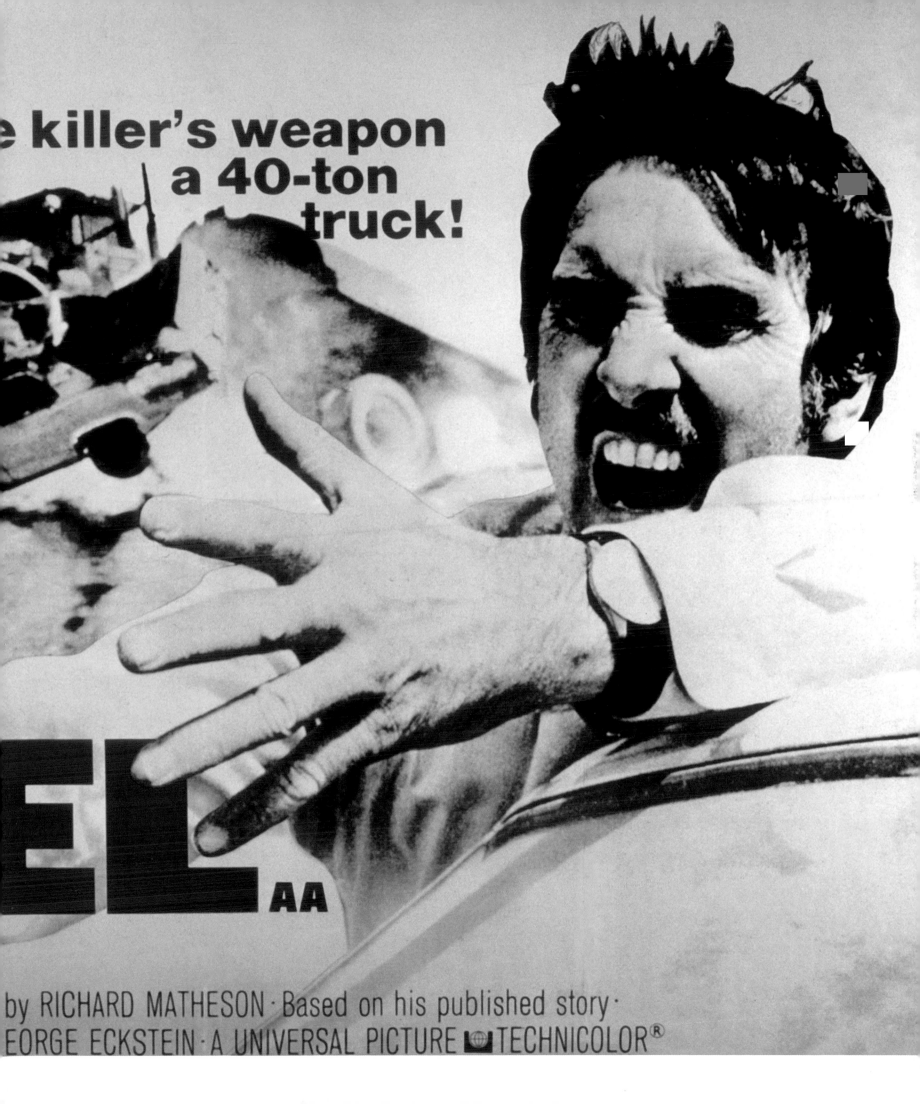

THE SUGARLAND EXPRESS

(1974)

"That's the one film that I can honestly say, if I had to do it all over again I'd make *Sugarland Express* in a completely different fashion."

Under starter's orders: The man whose first film, at the age of 13, was called *The Last Gun* demonstrates how to handle a pistol.

Previous page and left: In this second road movie, Goldie Hawn awaits direction as a nut job who turns into a folk heroine.

The Barwood-Robbins screenplay turned out rather well in Spielberg's judgment. He would receive at least two other serious offers (and a number of feelers) after the success of *Duel*, but this, he decided, would be his feature film debut. ("I might just have been in a four-wheel mode," Spielberg says now.) He took the script to Jennings Lang, who declared his love for it—but told Spielberg he could not greenlight the project unless he signed at least one major star to play one of the three principal roles: the woman determined to rescue her child from the toils of the Texas foster-care system, her husband, or the policeman who was leading the pursuit of the couple.

The true story of a girl who took on all of Texas and almost won.

A Zanuck/Brown Production

GOLDIE HAWN in
THE SUGARLAND EXPRESS

Co-starring Ben Johnson, Michael Sacks, William Atherton

Music by John Williams Screenplay by Hal Barwood & Matthew Robbins
Story by Steven Spielberg and Hal Barwood & Matthew Robbins
Directed by Steven Spielberg Produced by Richard D. Zanuck and David Brown
A Universal Picture Technicolor® Panavision® Distributed by Cinema International Corporation.

Zanuck and Brown, who had been assigned to produce the epic for Universal, agreed with Lang. They also agreed that the woman, whose role was frankly the best, would be the easiest to cast.

Spielberg, however, went after the male lead—specifically Jon Voight. They met at The Source on Sunset Boulevard, which owes its larger fame as the setting of Woody Allen's plea to Diane Keaton to return to New York with him at the end of *Annie Hall*. "He was a complete gentleman, but he passed at the end of lunch—because I was not experienced enough, I think that was basically it. He never said that, but I assume he was nervous that I was a first-time director."

It was time for Plan B. Zanuck and Brown proposed that Spielberg meet with Goldie Hawn. She was five years on from her Oscar-winning debut in *Cactus Flower*, and more years than that from the delightful dizziness of the *Laugh-In* television appearances. Her pictures after *Cactus Flower* had not been, on the whole, world-beaters. Spielberg met with her at her house, gave her the script and "she loved it, loved me, and she said yes."

So he had his Lou Jean Poplin, a woman who has lost custody of her child while serving a short jail term, and is, by God, going to get that baby back. She is the madly determined center of this movie—a nut job who somehow turns herself into a folk heroine as she pursues her quixotic role as the rescuer of her child. Spielberg did not need much else from his other actors. But William Atherton plays the role of Clovis, her somewhat clueless husband, with stolidity (or is it a dim awareness that this adventure is eventually going to go bad?), and his performance grounds the film in some sort of reality no one else wants to recognize. And the great Ben Johnson, three years on from *his* Oscar for *The Last Picture Show*, is a tolerant, patient, sympathetic, but ultimately betraying policeman.

All that really happens in the movie is a car chase that starts small and eventually grows huge. By its end what appears to be half the state of Texas is shadowing the couple and the very decent cop they have acquired as a hostage. Along the way, the mood of this mob subtly shifts. There is nothing wrong with the baby's situation; he is in the hands of a loving foster mom, who obviously will raise him in a more stable situation than Lou Jean and Clovis can provide.

But that's not the point as far as the trailing mob is concerned. Lou Jean is the baby's mother—all right, a mother who's had some bad luck—and by golly she is entitled to him, no matter that the State of Texas (and perhaps common sense) says otherwise. She becomes a populist heroine. And she revels in the role. By the end of the film we are justified in thinking that down-market celebrity has replaced compassion as her main driving force.

Goldie Hawn was a joy to work with: "She loved [the script], loved me, and she said yes."

"For me, anyway—nobody else sees it that way—but I think the heroes are the police, and I think the villains are the well-wishers that wished a little too much for these people."

> "It's a terrible indictment of the media more than anything else. It was a circus on wheels ... And I like the idea that today any one of us can create a major news story by doing the smallest, most simple neurotic act—which is sort of what this picture's about."

Above: The Poplins leave a trail of chaos as the adventure inevitably goes bad.

Previous page: Behind the scenes and in action with, among others, Goldie Hawn, Vilmos Zsigmond (wearing a hood), and William Atherton (in the front seat wearing a checked shirt).

"It did not escape me," says Spielberg, "that one of my favorite pictures of all time was *Ace in the Hole*," a 1951 Billy Wilder film which stressed the carnival atmosphere which grows around the story of a man trapped underground in a mine shaft—"the capitalization of that, the exploitation of that [situation], when I was sitting with Hal Barwood and Matthew Robbins working on the script" was very much on his mind. The hysteria is an important part of the movie's success, but it is allowed to grow quite organically in the film. It comes close to taking it over, but never quite does. This is perhaps due to Goldie Hawn's performance; she may be distracted at times by the hubbub growing around her, but she never lets us forget that, for her at least, there is serious, even heartbreaking business always at hand. "I thought she was an amazing actress for me to make my first film with—she was completely cooperative and she had a thousand good ideas."

At least as important was the scale of the film. Up to now, Spielberg's television shows had had relatively small casts and what spectacle he had provided was very much of the one-on-one variety (well-managed, of course), but here he had, eventually, hundreds of cars to wrangle and he did that with a cool expertise that was hugely impressive. The spectacle of the picture—casual but also palpable— was a factor in impressing the critics.

Spielberg and cinematographer Vilmos Zsigmond filming from the back of the insert vehicle.

"*Sugarland Express* did get good reviews, but I would have given away all those reviews for a bigger audience. The movie just broke even; it didn't make any money."

Pauline Kael at the *New Yorker*, for example, went completely overboard: "In terms of the pleasure that technical assurance gives an audience, this film is one of the most phenomenal debut films in the history of the movies." Most of the other reviews were in a similar vein. Some, Kael among them, worried that perhaps Spielberg was just another skilled entertainer in the Howard Hawks manner—though it is hard to say what was so bad about that. Neither she, nor anyone else as far as I can see, noticed that Spielberg here hinted at a theme that would loom larger and larger in his later films—the child who has become separated from his parents and who needs to find a resolution of some sort. Of course, in this instance that child is too young, too innocent, to know that he is lost and needs to be found.

Oddly enough, despite its critical reception, the film was not a notable commercial success. This is probably because it ends in muted tragedy; Clovis is shot when he is lured into retrieving the child. It is not a fate that we think he particularly deserves. It might also be that the film, essentially so good-natured, is nevertheless quite an exotic (or at least quirky) construct.

Spielberg was not of a mind to care too deeply about the film's commercial fate. It had done what it was supposed to; at a stroke it had made him credible as an A-list director.

In later years, he was inclined to think that the most important thing about *The Sugarland Express* was that it brought him in touch with his most significant, and longest-lasting, collaborator—the composer John Williams. When he was working on one of the rewrites for *Ace Eli and Rodger of the Skies*, he had stumbled across a recording of the score for *The Reivers*, a film by Mark Rydell. "I wore that LP out," Spielberg says. "When I turned in my third draft, I said, 'I don't care what happens to this movie, but when I make my first feature, whoever this guy is, I want him to write the score.'" He did, of course—and for virtually every Spielberg movie since then. It is, without a doubt, the longest-running director–composer relationship in the history of the movies.

That was all in the future. For the moment, it was enough that he had proved himself more than capable of handling large forces in a suspenseful fashion. And Zanuck and Brown now held the rights to a best-selling novel that seemed to be perfect for him. Which, as it happened, was correct. The only problem was that before he was finished with *Jaws* it would pose the largest threat to his career that it ever endured.

JAWS

(1975)

"*Jaws* was my Vietnam. It was basically naïve people against nature, and nature beat us every day."

"It's a visceral film. It's a horror film that's going to tear your guts out. *The Exorcist* made you vomit, and this film will make you clutch your hands to your armpits."

Jaws began life as a not particularly promising project by the journeyman writer Peter Benchley, grandson of the delicious humorist and actor Robert Benchley. It is said that he sold it to his publisher on the basis of a one-page outline for $1,000. It is, most basically, a knock-off of the Ibsen play *An Enemy of the People*, in which a resort town tries to cover up the fact that its spa, the center of its tourist business, is polluted. The play recounts the efforts of a single just man to uncover this inconvenient truth and the efforts of the town fathers to silence him and preserve the profitable status quo. It is a very solid, well-constructed work. It was Benchley's conceit to re-stage this drama in a Massachusetts seaside resort and to put a menacing zing into the story by replacing the polluted spa with—well, let's say it—a shark.

From the scene board to the poster and props, the overwhelming motif for the movie was jagged teeth.

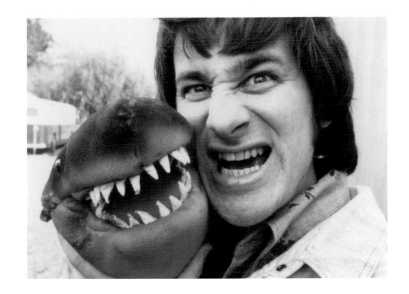

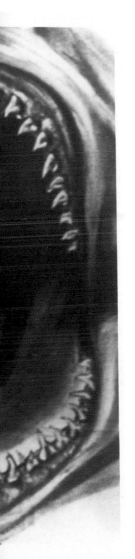

And not just any shark. It had to be a huge—and very malevolent—creature from the deep, one whose presence could be hidden from the populace for only a certain amount of time and who is believed in, at first, by only three men: Sam Quint (Robert Shaw), a half-mad survivor of the shark attack on the sailors of the USS *Indianapolis* after their ship was sunk during World War II, and whose interest in this shark is highly personal; Matt Hooper (Richard Dreyfuss), an ironic marine biologist who is Quint's opposite, rational and scientific; and Martin Brody (Roy Scheider), the town cop and a sort of everyman, seeking some sort of practical solution to a problem that just won't go away.

Benchley's book is, in its way, quite well written. It does not particularly indulge in hysteria—until finally it must, as the attacks grow more public and more horrendous. In any event, the book struck a chord with the public. By the time Zanuck and Brown acquired the property (for the relatively low price of $175,000 with Benchley's services as a screenwriter thrown in), the book was well on its way to selling some five and a half million copies—with more to come, of course, when the movie was released. Legend has it that Spielberg plucked a copy of an early script off a pile in the Zanuck-Brown office, read it over a weekend and returned the following Monday hopped up to make the movie. He was not unaware that the story bore a certain resemblance to *Duel*, with the shark, of course, standing in for the unseen truck driver. Indeed, by this time he had acquired a *Duel* poster—from the Polish release of the film— that "had the truck with a huge mouth, like a shark, so it looked like it was about to scoop up the car. So it wasn't just me who noticed that."

Alas for Spielberg, another director, Dick Richards, was attached to the film at that point. In a few weeks, however, the competitor dropped out. *Jaws* was now Spielberg's—for better or for worse. In its making it was pretty much for the worse, legendarily so.

The first question was, of course, where to make it. Shooting on open water is always a vexing question. No director who has done it has ever repeated the experience. Water is ever changing—in light, in the condition of the sea, in the utter uncontrollability of all the elements in the environment. Essentially, you cannot match shots. Or, rather you can—if you have the time and patience to do so. And, of course, the money.

The studio was all for building a tank on the back lot, so that Spielberg could manage the hydraulics of the situation. "I said no," he recalls. "I want to go out and battle the elements. I want people to think this is really happening; that shark is really in the ocean and I want a real ocean. I don't want this to look like *The Old Man and the Sea*, with the painted background and the cycloramas and all of that"—basically screaming movie fakery in every shot.

So off they went, a cast and crew of some two hundred people descending on Martha's Vineyard, all raring to go. And at first it went pretty well. There were lots of sequences set on dry land, which were relatively easy to do—certainly within the range of normal moviemaking. Basically, Spielberg was blowing off his cover shots—the pieces directors normally save to shoot on the days when more complicated location shots can't be accomplished because of weather or technical problems. He noticed that he was doing so, but he was not abnormally concerned. What could go wrong?

Almost everything, it turned out—beginning with the regattas. All summer long people are racing sailboats off Martha's Vineyard, and you have to wait for them to clear the horizon because you can't make a scary movie with a shark menacing three guys in a boat and assorted landlubbers when there are dozens of pleasure boats sailing peaceably by seven miles away. And, of course, the farther away they are the longer it takes for them to clear the shot— not to mention that Spielberg was shooting in wide screen; at a normal aspect ratio they would have been out of shot much sooner than in this one. Whole mornings would be lost before they got a clear horizon.

By which time underwater currents would almost invariably have dragged the anchors of the film boats— the camera boat, the generator, the shark barge—out of position and as much as two and a half hours would be spent restoring them to their original places. By then, of course, it was lunch time—without a shot being made. This routine would typically be repeated in the afternoon. Spielberg was used to going home at 7pm with perhaps one shot to show for a day's work. Sometimes none.

It was, if nothing else, tedious—"the mosquitoes came 12 miles out just to bite you," Spielberg remembers.

Meantime, back at the studio people were beginning to notice that costs were mounting. On location, rumors of Spielberg's replacement were beginning to circulate. What hopes Spielberg had of keeping his job and finishing the picture now rested with "Bruce," as the shark had been nicknamed. If it could perform "like Esther Williams" the picture might yet be saved—or at least lived through. On the 38th day of shooting—it was a Sunday—Bruce was ready for its first camera test. And with Zanuck and Brown in the boat with Spielberg, they cranked up the shark. It was supposed to breach the water, which it did. "It came right out perfectly. And then the head kind of went down like a submarine. And then the tail sort of fell over the other way, there was an explosion of bubbles and another, then it was eerily quiet—we were actually witnessing the shark sinking to the bottom of the ocean." The producers optimistically guessed the shark would be repaired by the next morning. The word came back that it would not be ready for its close-up for another three or four weeks.

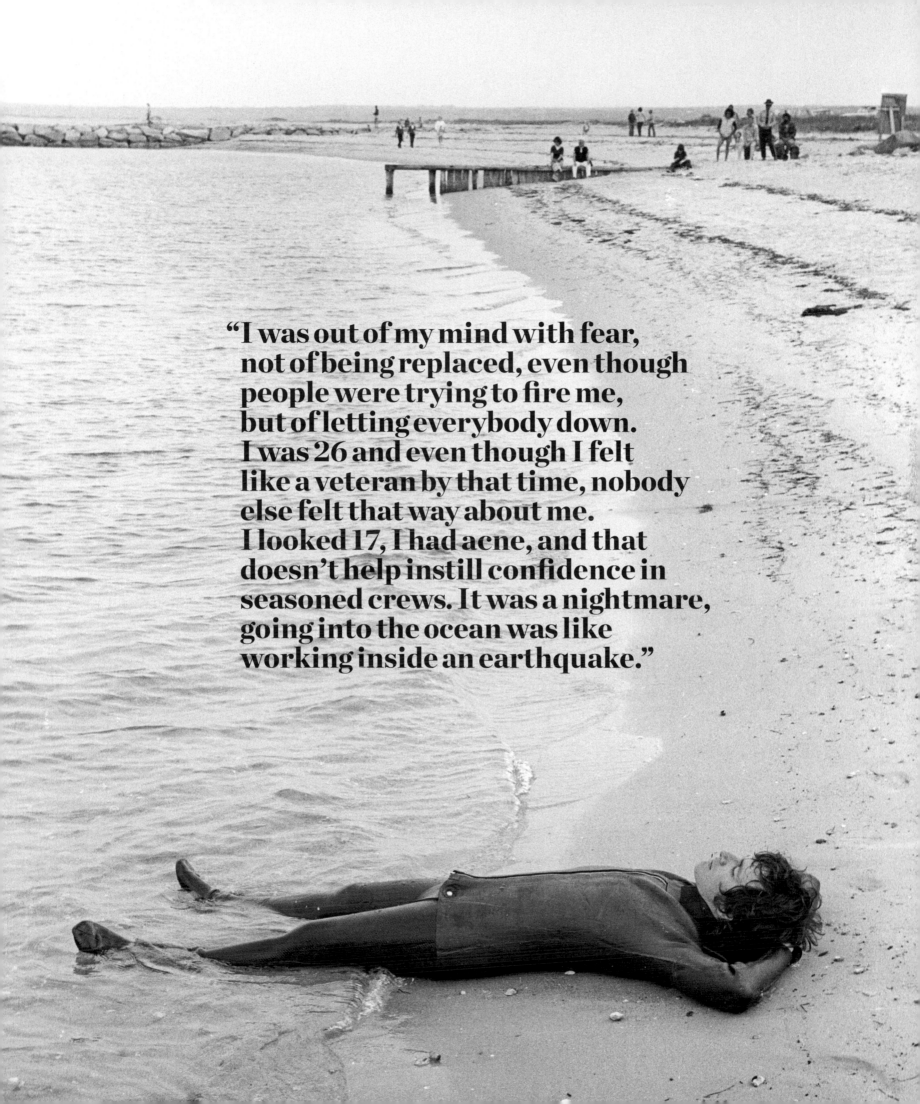

"I was out of my mind with fear,
not of being replaced, even though
people were trying to fire me,
but of letting everybody down.
I was 26 and even though I felt
like a veteran by that time, nobody
else felt that way about me.
I looked 17, I had acne, and that
doesn't help instill confidence in
seasoned crews. It was a nightmare,
going into the ocean was like
working inside an earthquake."

"I'm not so much afraid of sharks, I'm afraid of the water and I'm afraid of everything that exists under the water that I can't see."

Right: A rare moment of peace (top) and testing "Bruce" as an air mattress (bottom).

Opposite: Richard Dreyfuss, Roy Scheider, and Robert Shaw struggle to keep the *Orca* afloat, but the shark prevails.

Below: The suitably framed protagonists, Robert Shaw, Roy Scheider, and Richard Dreyfuss.

Previous page: Terrified bathers respond to a shark alert (main image) as Spielberg keeps a calmer head, directing the extras (top) and even editing in situ (bottom).

It was time for Plan B. But Spielberg didn't, off hand, have a Plan B. By Monday he had one, "which was basically suggesting the shark without showing the shark—not in full anyway." It was a matter of a fin here, a tail there, a nose somewhere else—combined, of course, in the finished picture, with John Williams' brilliant shark theme. The audience doesn't get a full view of the thing until Roy Scheider is chumming for it and it appears in its full monstrous glory. "You wouldn't have had that shock if the shark had been used too often and too clearly before that."

All well and good in the final analysis. But the final analysis was still a long way off in the summer of 1974. What Spielberg was doing was very subtle, and to a large degree dependent on the aforementioned music and, of course, on Verna Fields' brilliant editing.

He had his supporters, of course—Dick Zanuck and David Brown had threatened to quit the picture if he was fired. And Sid Sheinberg made, as it were, a fish-or-cut-bait visit to the location. He sat Spielberg down on the steps of the hotel where the crew was staying and said: "Look, this is a disaster.

I don't know what to do, except we could pull the plug right now. We could take our losses. We could all go back to Los Angeles and never, ever make a movie called *Jaws* again. Maybe we could put the shark on the tour on the back lot and make a few bucks back."

But he said, "I'm going to let you make the call. You can fold up shop right now and nobody will replace you. You won't be fired. I will simply cancel the entire production, 'cause this may be impossible. This may be the one film that's too impossible to make. Or you can go ahead and stick with it and I'll back you a hundred percent."

Spielberg, without hesitation, said he would stick with it. It was not mere bravado speaking. I think his filmmaker's instinct was telling him that he had finally found the right path. It was not just a matter of keeping the monster confined largely to the shadows. It was also, as important, keeping its appearances brief when it finally did show up.

"I think the shark not working when we needed it to probably added $175 million to the box office—because what's scary about the movie is the unseen, not what we see."

The company finally left Martha's Vineyard in the early fall of 1974—with work still to be done. There were pickups still to be made—on the Pacific shore rather than the Atlantic. And Verna Fields still had her editing magic to apply. She would, says Spielberg "surgically cut a frame off the head of the shark and cut a frame off the tail of the shark and those two frames made the difference between the shark looking like a 26-foot long predator or it looking like a 26-foot long turd."

But, at last—more than a hundred days over schedule, and radically over budget—*Jaws* was finished. And, miracle upon miracle, it was something to behold. It was perhaps the soundness of the story that triumphed over all. "It's a pretty good story, a pretty perfect structure," he says now, and that purely visceral appeal is what the press responded to when the picture began screening in the early summer of 1975. If the shark is a perfect eating machine, *Jaws* was about to turn into a perfect money-making machine.

It was helped in that regard by what was, in those days, an unusual marketing method. From time immemorial

movies (with the exception of a few horror movies) had been released in a tried-and-tested manner: downtown theaters premiering them in the major markets, followed by a slowish spread to sub-runs in the outlying districts. It was not uncommon for a picture to go out with perhaps 50 prints for the whole country. *Jaws* was different—over 400 prints were struck. It was everywhere on its first weekend. This is now common practice—most big movies today routinely go out with 2,000 (or more) prints on their opening weekend, their fates essentially sealed by the end of Sunday night. Which was true of *Jaws*. It was a mighty hit. Very shortly it became clear that it was about to become the biggest-grossing movie of all time—$260 million in domestic revenues alone.

That record would soon be surpassed—just two years later his friend George Lucas's *Star Wars* would be the first of many movies to do so. Yet Spielberg still stands in somewhat ambivalent relationship to the film: "I credit *Jaws* with everything. I'm completely grateful that the audience embraced the movie and that the movie became such a

phenomenon, which basically gave me what I had dreamed about—being a movie director and having the final cut—you know, [being able] to tie my own noose. It gave me freedom. And I've never lost my freedom."

And yet, in some sense, it scarred him—mildly, to be sure, but memorably. "The experience of making *Jaws* was horrendous for me." Up to then, his experiences as a young director had been pretty standard—mild triumphs, mild setbacks, but basically a steady growth to mastery. This time, though, it was different—the scale of difficulty, the unanticipated problems, the sense that all eyes were watching, was pretty close to overwhelming. Many directors, perhaps most of them, never encounter that kind of pressure in careers that extend for decades. For all that the film gave him, he became, not cautious, but in a sense careful. He would never again go into production on a film without having all his bases covered.

Many years later, in 1998, when the American Film Institute issued its first list of the one hundred greatest American films, Spielberg found himself with five pictures

Audiences queued round the block to see *Jaws* (here at the Rivoli theater, New York). But, even with an extra pair of hands, for Spielberg the effort involved in making the film proved almost intolerable.

among the chosen few. He called the Institute to ask if possibly *Jaws* could be dropped from their number. He doesn't make much of that request—he just thought that there were other, worthier movies that deserved recognition, and that he had more than enough of that without *Jaws* being listed. The request was denied, and Spielberg makes light of it. He contents himself with wryly saying "You've probably noticed I haven't done very many water pictures since *Jaws*."

"My next picture will be made on dry land. There won't even be a bathroom scene."

CLOSE ENCOUNTERS OF THE THIRD KIND

(1977)

"If you believe, it's science fact;
if you don't believe, it's science
fiction. I'm an agnostic between
the two beliefs, so for me it's
science speculation."

"Richard Dreyfuss has been me in three movies. He's been my doppelgänger in a sense—the only actor I've ever kind of identified with, perceived myself to be." It is a matter of tenacity and ambition, Spielberg thinks—qualities Dreyfuss is certainly not lacking. "He looks for answers and he's got energy, he talks fast and he moves fast, and he's not 6'4" which is a height I've always wanted to be and will never achieve. And he's cute." He's also not particularly fearful of water, which Spielberg somewhat is—a virtue that obviously came in handy on *Jaws*. "And he's easy to write for. It's easy to put myself in his shoes and say 'If I was him this is what I'd do, but I'll let him do it, so I don't have to.'"

Previous page: On the set of *Close Encounters*, and finding his heart in the right place.

In short, he was perfectly cast as Roy Neary in *Close Encounters*. Roy is a rather ordinary fellow, trapped in a rather ordinary job, and slightly unhappy in it—looking, pretty much unconsciously, for a transcendent experience, but not at all certain what that experience might be. He is, not to put too fine a point on it, a childlike figure, who, of course, finds his way to a huge, secret government project, set up at the "Devil's Tower" in Wyoming, broadcasting a musical signal—one of John Williams' most inspired themes—into space. The signal is supposed to tell space aliens that they will find a warm welcome should they descend to earth and make contact with its inhabitants. "I came up with the idea of doing it through music as opposed to 'take me to your leader' subtitles because it becomes a little bit of a mystery you have to uncover— five notes of a grand opera between the extra-terrestrials and the human race."

It is really quite a simple story, though it is pleasantly complicated by the presence of a child whose innocent curiosity is driving him as surely as Roy is driven by a slightly more complicated desire for understanding. The film is also enlivened by a very agreeable sense of humor; Roy keeps getting enigmatic clues that he is on the track of something real and important. (Who can forget him modeling Devil's Tower out of a pile of mashed potatoes?)

Spielberg in conversation with composer John Williams, his long-standing collaborator. *Close Encounters* was unusual in that Williams composed the score first and the film was edited to fit, rather than vice versa.

Devil's Tower looms behind Richard Dreyfuss, François Truffaut, and Teri Garr.

Overleaf: The iconic mountain in Wyoming has almost as much screen time as any of the principals.

That Roy finally attains his goal, to encounter the aliens' huge space vehicle (as does François Truffaut, the project leader, who has a communications problem of his own, in that he does not speak English) and eventually decides to board it, is perhaps a foregone conclusion, but hardly, in the context of this film, an unhappy one.

Spielberg was, as a child, mildly dyslexic, thus not much of a reader. But there was an exception: science fiction. His father was an avid reader of magazines like *Amazing Stories* and his son soon shared his enthusiasm for them. It was the same with movies. More than westerns or war stories he was drawn to sci-fi, which was more than understandable: The 1950s was the first great age for this genre.

He developed particular tastes within the genre. He preferred, for example, films in which invaders from outer space came to earth, as opposed to earthlings venturing out among the stars—all of his projects in this form have been of this character. Also, the visitors have been relatively benign (with the exception, of course, of those in *War of the Worlds*). His father had made a simple telescope that he and Steven

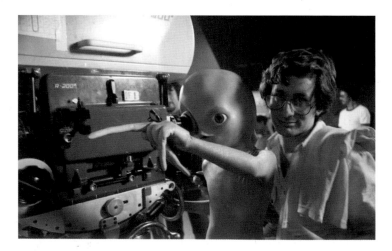

used to study the stars, and, peering though it, Spielberg couldn't imagine "being attacked by those wonders of the universe. It was, for me, a journey into discovery. I didn't feel anxious. I didn't feel a threat from up there. I always looked up at the sky and just saw all sorts of wonders. So to me it was inconceivable that if I did get into science fiction someday my first movie would be aggressive."

Other factors shaped his taste as well. For instance, he noticed in many science-fiction stories that children are more receptive to, well, close encounters of the third kind. While their parents run around and call the FBI, the kids approach aliens with openness and wonder. As in so many of his movies, their main desire is to begin communications, have a dialogue with whatever has stopped by for a visit.

This he turned into something like a cosmic problem for the purposes of his film. In 1974, when Spielberg was writing *Close Encounters*, he "somehow felt that with the Cold War and the Russians not talking to the Americans, and with Watergate and Nixon about to be impeached, there seemed to be a huge communications abyss. *Close Encounters* was my first sort of attempt to send out a message that if we can communicate with aliens then why can't we communicate with each other. For me, it's one of the most hopeful movies I've ever written and directed."

It is also one of the slyest. Take just one example: At some point close to the end of the film, the alien mother ship disgorges some of its passengers, whose numbers include all of the famous people who have disappeared from the face of the earth (Amelia Earhart, Judge Crater, et al.). They all are at the age they were when they vanished. And they all appear to be perfectly happy. Which is another earnest message, if any is needed, that the aliens don't have a mean bone in their bodies—not entirely a first in pictures of this kind, but certainly rare enough.

The director, at the center of the film on set in the massive dirigible hangars (above) and on location in India (opposite); and accepting alien assistance behind the camera (below).

"*Jaws* is a movie I could have played on a toy xylophone, but *Close Encounters* made me stretch further, it required all 88 keys."

Just as in *E.T.* five years later, it is children who have some of the closest encounters with the extra-terrestrial visitors. One boy in particular, Barry Guiler (played by Cary Guffey), is carried off in the aliens' mother ship (above) before being returned safe and well. Here he is also shown bathed in the strange nocturnal light that heralds the aliens' arrival (left); with his mother Jillian, played by Melinda Dillon (opposite, top); and trying out the director's baseball cap for size (opposite, bottom).

"I really believe that *Close Encounters* was probably the closest I've ever come to achieving a dream on film."

As Spielberg says, "Here's the message: If you have any ambition about learning more about yourself, you're going to follow your God-given instincts and you're going to follow all the signs and you're going to go to the place where the party's going to occur and you're going to have a chance to commune with—whatever we have to offer you. That's really as simple as the story is."

And it was, for all its impressive set pieces, a relatively easy picture to shoot. Spielberg was working with Julia and Michael Phillips, coming off their huge success with *The Sting*, and the picture was set up at Columbia, which was, at the time, in relatively dire financial straits, but he reports no interference from anyone—just a certain amount of manageable anxiety. Today, well after the fact, he wonders if in the last analysis he would have had Dreyfuss opt to sail off into space with the aliens. "I wrote the story in my late twenties, and I don't think today, being a dad with seven kids, I would have let my Richard Dreyfuss character actually get on the mother ship and abandon his family to this alien obsession and leave the planet."

On the other hand, at the time "it was something that absolutely would have been my choice—get me on that mother ship. I want to explore along with those guys."

Certainly George Lucas agreed with Spielberg. The encounter with the alien ship was not shot outdoors—too many variables to contend with—but in two disused World War II dirigible hangars. Bigger than a couple of football fields and many times larger than any Hollywood sound stage. Lucas, having completed principal photography on *Star Wars*, and highly dubious about what he had wrought (he has always said that he didn't begin to fully appreciate his achievement until John Williams' score was added to the movie), dropped by for a visit. He was duly impressed; he didn't think he had anything in his picture that could match this mighty spaceship. Spielberg, of course, demurred. He thought the Lucas film was going to be an enormous hit—just wait and see.

At some point, Lucas in effect said put your money where your mouth is. Let's trade points in each other's films—2.5 of them to be exact. Their lawyers did the deal. In which, obviously, no one got hurt. *Close Encounters* was a substantial hit. But *Star Wars*, of course, was a monster hit (two years later it replaced *Jaws* as the biggest movie success of all time). Not without a certain wry satisfaction, Spielberg notes that, to this day, he still receives checks for his share of participation in the film.

Below:
"Get me on that mother ship." At the time he wrote the story, Spielberg would have made the same choice as Dreyfuss's character—to fly away with the aliens.

Opposite: "We are not alone." Truffaut as French scientist Lacombe opens communications with Curwen hand signs (top, left). "You belong here more than me." The small aliens in the final scenes were played by local girls in Mobile, Alabama (top, right).

1941

(1979)

"What happened on the screen was pretty out of control, but the production was pretty much in control. I don't dislike the movie at all. I'm not embarrassed by it—I just think that it wasn't funny enough."

The picture opens with a send-up of a famous scene in *Jaws*; a pretty girl (Susan Backlinie) runs down a beach, shedding her robe and plunges into the water, where she ends up not assaulted by a shark, but clinging naked to the periscope of an emerging Japanese submarine. The imitation of the scene was perfect in terms of staging, lighting, and, in its way, shock value. It was even the same actress. The preview audience in Dallas rocked with laughter. "Eight hundred people couldn't stop laughing," and standing at the back of the house Steven Spielberg thought, "Oh my God, I have a comedy hit."

Previous page: (From left to right) Dan Aykroyd, Mickey Rourke, John Candy, Treat Williams, and Walter Olkewicz give their verdict. One of them was right.

Soon the screen will be bombarded by the
most explosive barrage of 痛快 ever filmed.

UNIVERSAL PICTURES and COLUMBIA PICTURES Present
An A-Team Production of
A STEVEN SPIELBERG FILM

1941

DAN AYKROYD · NED BEATTY · JOHN BELUSHI · LORRAINE GARY · MURRAY HAMILTON
CHRISTOPHER LEE · TIM MATHESON · TOSHIRO MIFUNE · WARREN OATES · ROBERT STACK · TREAT WILLIAMS
NANCY ALLEN · EDDIE DEEZEN · BOBBY DiCICCO · DIANNE KAY · SLIM PICKENS · WENDIE JO SPERBER · LIONEL STANDER
Director of Photography WILLIAM A. FRAKER, A.S.C. Screenplay by ROBERT ZEMECKIS & BOB GALE
Story by ROBERT ZEMECKIS & BOB GALE and JOHN MILIUS Music by JOHN WILLIAMS
Produced by BUZZ FEITSHANS Executive Producer JOHN MILIUS
Directed by STEVEN SPIELBERG   Read the Ballantine Book

With its expensively constructed sets,
frenetic pace, and "explosive barrage" of
mayhem, *1941* had all the ingredients of a
major comedy hit—except for the comedy.

Overleaf: "I just blew too much stuff up."

Not so fast, Buddy. "The second that scene was over, and the
actual movie began, there were about four laughs in the next
two hours." With *1941*, Spielberg was on his way to the worst
critical drubbing of his life. He still wonders, occasionally,
what went wrong—though in the longer perspective he is
inclined to think it was among the best things that ever
happened to him.

The script was by Robert Zemeckis and Bob Gale with
the inspirational assistance of John Milius, who functioned
as executive producer on the project. It was based, very
loosely, on a real incident. In the immediate aftermath of
Pearl Harbor, a Japanese submarine had indeed surfaced
near Santa Barbara, and lobbed a few shells into an oil
refinery there, sowing panic in Southern California. The film
extrapolates from that event and has the pilot of an airplane
(fictionally involved in the incident and played by John
Belushi) heading for Hollywood with intent to bomb what
he conceives of as the true capital of the American spirit.
Nothing ensues from his misadventures but pure madness;
not one of the Americans responding to his further activities
is anything but crazy or stupid or both.

Spielberg judged the script brilliant, about the funniest such document he had ever read, and he set to work realizing it with a high and happy heart. He had his setbacks. For example, he asked John Wayne, whose acquaintance he had made at a memorial service for Joan Crawford, to play General Joseph Stilwell, the only historical character in the film. Wayne called him back almost immediately urging him not to do the picture, on the grounds that it was Un-American, which was nonsense, and on the grounds that Spielberg was "better than that," which was undoubtedly true (in the end the part was played, with nicely judged incomprehension, by Robert Stack).

The real problem with the film perhaps began with Spielberg's misplaced passion for the project, which contained a sort of hubris. Everything had worked out so beautifully for him to that point. Now he could pursue an impossible perfectionism, which no one dared question, let alone deny. "I've got to perfect every angle. I've got to wait for the right light. I've got to wait until John Belushi and Dan Aykroyd are in the right mood, although they were always in the right mood."

That spirit extended to every aspect of the production— "I just became so precious and indulgent about getting everything right. I did 20 takes on inserts that should have been done by a second unit. I directed every miniature. I should have had a miniature crew come in and shoot the Ferris wheel rolling down the pier. I had a first unit company, being paid first unit dollars, shooting that."

It was not, he says, that he "misbehaved. I didn't. I had my temper tantrums, my little angry outbursts," but they didn't amount to much. It was just that all this fussing was costly. In the end the picture took longer to make than *Jaws*—and it was shot mainly on sound stages, not on location.

And it was over-produced. And noisy. "I think what killed the comedy was the amount of destruction, and the sheer noise level. I often describe *1941* as having your head stuck in a pinball machine while somebody is hitting tilt over and over again." At that Dallas preview many people were watching the film with their hands over their ears because they were being assaulted by all the noise coming out of the speakers. "It's not that we dubbed it too loud, I just blew too much stuff up."

Close encounter with a T. rex. The critics'
response to Spielberg's fifth feature was
to be equally ferocious.

Indubitably, but one must say that when moviemakers are insecure about a film, there is a tendency, conscious or unconscious, to crank up the volume to force acquiescence in the merriment. That, however, is a relatively minor problem. Successful movie comedy is, far more often than not, a product of relative poverty. Chaplin's dictum that he could make a funny picture with no more elements than a park, a girl, a cop, and a relatively addled boy is a truism. It applies to everyone from the Marx Brothers to Woody Allen. When a large cast or outside ambition or, heaven forbid, a wide range of machinery intrudes, laughter sooner or later dies. As it did here.

In the early summer of 1979, six or seven months before the picture's opening, Spielberg joined Pauline Kael on a radio show she was then hosting. During a break in the proceedings, she mentioned *1941* to Spielberg and said, as he recalls, "Well, we're all waiting for that one. You're not going to get off as easy as you did on your first ones—we're waiting for you to fail."

That was the kind of thing Kael was wont to do—she liked to send little shivers of fear through people, even those she considered friends, and Spielberg flinched. In fact, Kael gave *1941* a positive review, while most critics disliked the film. They were not alone—audiences loathed it as well. Today, Spielberg considers the lesson salutary. However, he can't help but salvage some pride in the film. Curiously, it did rather well with reviewers and audiences in some foreign territories—France, Germany, Japan, for instance. The view there, essentially, was that the all-American filmmaker had made something like an anti-American film—which was far from his intention. He was—no kidding—just trying to be funny in a farcical vein, which was, putting it mildly, not his strong suit. Nor was it one to which he ever returned.

He does observe that many years later the picture finally broke even—in the circumstances, some kind of modest, if not entirely consoling, outcome. What was finally, perhaps, the most important thing to happen on the production was his introduction to Kathleen Kennedy, then working as an assistant to John Milius. The two bonded, and she quite quickly became his line producer and, more than that, his trusted confidante—a position she continues to hold and carries with great distinction.

RAIDERS OF THE LOST ARK

(1981)

"George pitched me the story, and I committed on the beach. We started a tradition of building lucky sandcastles. So we used to build sandcastles in Hawaii, and if the sandcastle withstood the first high tide, the film was a hit. If the high tide overran the sandcastle, we were going to have to struggle to make our money back."

In May of 1977 Spielberg was in Hawaii to hold George Lucas's hand (metaphorically speaking). Lucas's wife, Marcia, a gifted film editor, "had his right hand, I had his left hand, waiting for the phone to ring." The incoming call would report grosses on the first morning's showings of *Star Wars*. There was really nothing to worry about; the picture's early screenings had been sensational. The film had come out of nowhere, a fairly modestly budgeted science-fiction epic (for want of a better term) that also touched lightly and wittily on some of the *ur*-themes that Joseph Campbell and others had adumbrated in works like *The Hero with a Thousand Faces*.

With George Lucas, trying to stay in the shade on location in Tunisia, and (previous page) at a tribal gathering with the Hovitos, in Hawaii.

Beneath its non-stop action and wisecracking dialogue, the picture spoke of Luke Skywalker's coming of age and, more importantly perhaps, of his search for a lost father who had gone over to "the dark side." It had, in short, a kind of shallow depth that was not common in sci-fi, but that in no way interfered with the sheer fun of the thing.

Spielberg thought his friend had nothing to worry about, though neither he nor anyone else predicted the phenomenon *Star Wars* was about to become. "George wasn't talking much the night before," he says, but then the phone call came. The picture had sold out every single one of its 10:30am screenings, all across the nation. Euphoria replaced the anxious gloom that had surrounded the island retreat, "and in his euphoria he immediately began thinking about the future." This included Steven Spielberg's future, about which Spielberg was, uncharacteristically, uncertain. He had previously approached Albert "Cubby" Broccoli, proprietor of the hugely successful James Bond franchise, about directing an episode in that series and had been rebuffed. But he was thinking of trying again.

It is, frankly, hard to see why. The Bond pictures are essentially soulless—all action and no substance, lots of spectacular action sequences, some cynical and repetitive dialogue, making them little more than machine-made money-spinning enterprises. It perhaps speaks to Spielberg's youth (he was just turning 30 in 1977) that he did not fully understand where his greatest strengths lay.

George Lucas did. At some point later in their Hawaiian stay he said to Spielberg, "I've got something better than James Bond, it's called *Raiders of the Lost Ark*." Actually he didn't have it—not in the full sense of the term. He had a central character, originally called Indiana Smith, and he had an image of him—fedora, leather jacket, maybe the whip—and the idea for a quest: something about the adventurous archaeologist trying to recover "The Lost Ark of the Covenant."

"I should have known a lot more about it, because I'm Jewish and George isn't. But George knew a lot of the history of when it went missing, and what the mythology was about it." Other than that, they had nothing. "Everything else had not been worked out."

In retrospect, we can see that the film was, essentially, the *Star Wars* format reset in an entirely different time and place with an obviously different plot. There was the non-stop action, the wisecracks, an underlying large theme, though not anywhere near as mythically powerful as that of the earlier picture. And, of course, in the event there was once again Harrison Ford—that grumbling, distant, occasionally risible figure, almost (but not quite) subversive, almost (but not quite) an anti-hero.

Marion: "You're not the man I knew 10 years ago." Indiana: "It's not the years, honey, it's the mileage." A close encounter with Harrison Ford with Karen Allen attempting to intervene.

"I want the audience to know not only which side the good guy's on and the bad guy's on, but which side of the screen they're in, and I want the audience to be able to edit as quickly as they want in a shot that I am loath to cut away from. And that's been my style with all four of these Indiana Jones pictures."

The picture did not begin to come together until Spielberg found, more or less under his nose, the screenwriter, Lawrence Kasdan, who had written *Continental Divide*, which Spielberg executive-produced for Universal. Spielberg introduced Kasdan to Lucas, and the three of them spent three days in a little house in the Valley, where they essentially plotted the whole picture, at least to the point where Kasdan could go off and write the script, which he did while *1941* was filming. Indeed, Spielberg received the first review of that film on his first day of shooting *Raiders* at La Rochelle, France, site of a still photographically viable Nazi submarine pen. It was a favorable notice from Pauline Kael, the only such endorsement Spielberg claims he received from an American reviewer.

1941 was, of course, his first—but far from last—involvement with World War II, and, like *Raiders*, was far from a serious study of a subject his father introduced him to as a child. The elder Spielberg had been a B-25 radio operator in Burma, and had enjoyed "a good war" there. His stories enthralled the young Steven, who had made some of his little 8mm films about the war. Oddly enough, only *1941* and the great later film *Empire of the Sun* touched on the war with the Japanese, and neither of them had anything to do with his father's war.

But he had learned a costly lesson from *1941*. And George Lucas reinforced it. "'Look, you can go over schedule for Columbia and Universal, but you're my friend. You can't go over schedule with the money I'm responsible for.' That's all he had to say."

With his trademark fedora, grumbling wisecracks, and nose for danger, Indiana Jones was to become one of cinema's best-loved action heroes.

Horsemanship and ability to handle a bullwhip were just two of the skills Harrison Ford needed to play the role of Indiana Jones.

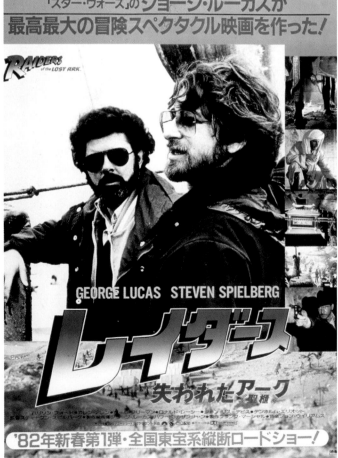

Right:
Snakes, snakes,
and more snakes,
"The whole place
is slitherin'!"

"We had 7,000 live snakes. We began with 3,000 and it didn't look like enough, then we had 5,000 rubber snakes and the rubber snakes were controlled by wires. But with not many controllers and more snakes, they had to put 100 snakes on every wire, so it was kind of like watching the June Taylor Dancers. They were all—hundreds were—moving at the same time and it didn't work."

Lucas's words hit home. "I was humbled," Spielberg says. "Every single shot was storyboarded. I was 14 days under schedule—something like that. He wasn't on the set. He wasn't over my shoulder. He was having his life up north and I was having mine. He came to visit sometimes, but he wasn't haunting me, he wasn't my on-set producer. I think *Raiders* was probably the most prepared I've ever been to direct a movie, and it paid off."

In its way, *Raiders* is a perfect adventure film, a headlong series of incidents that does not pause to dither over plausibility. Lucas, as he had already proved in *Star Wars*, had always loved the serials of the 1930s and 40s (*Don Winslow of the Navy* and *Flash Gordon* had been particular influences on that film) and Spielberg was at least knowledgeable about the lowbrow tradition they were working in. Their movie satirized it, but never trashed it. It keeps an ironic distance from it—costuming, dialogue, impossible situations fallen into and escaped from, a cheeky woman (Karen Allen, undaunted by the seemingly endless

peril in which she finds herself). This, combined with the discipline, fiscal and otherwise, with which the picture was made, combined to make it among the happiest of Spielberg's films, although, truth to tell, he has never had unhappy shoots.

Perhaps only one thing worried him. The picture opens with a sort of prequel—it has nothing to do with the subsequent story—in which Indy is escaping from an underground cavern—lots of nasty snakes and insects, and a huge ball of rock nipping at his heel. It is an utterly thrilling sequence. When he showed the film at industry screenings, a couple of his director pals worried that the movie would never top the thrills inherent in that opening. My God, he said to himself in effect, the entire rest of the film is going to suffer by comparison.

That, of course, did not happen. The film bounced along most wonderfully—and profitably. And there were, of course, sequels to come—which, by and large, maintained the standards of the original.

Opposite: *Raiders* was a global smash, grossing $384 million worldwide. The iconic English-language poster (top, left), and other examples from Mexico (top, right), Japan (bottom, left), and Poland (bottom, right).

E.T.
THE EXTRA-TERRESTRIAL
(1982)

"When I started *E.T.* I was fat and happy and satisfied with having the films I had on my list. And I just didn't feel I had anything to lose. I had nothing to prove to anybody except me."

One of the great strengths of *E.T.* is the performances by its child stars, particularly that of Henry Thomas as Elliott, a projection of Spielberg.

Spielberg thinks perhaps the root idea for *E.T.* lies buried in his childhood, when he was "a little, little kid, feeling somewhat lost and alienated and being this Jewish kid always in all-gentile neighborhoods." This sense of alienation was reinforced when he was 16 and his parents split up, which, despite his comparative maturity, he took very hard, again feeling very much "lost and alone." That, at any rate, was the germ of the idea he discussed with Melissa Mathison on the set of *Raiders of the Lost Ark* in Tunisia when they were shooting there in the summer of 1980. She was, at the time, Harrison Ford's girlfriend. More important to Spielberg, she had been co-screenwriter on *The Black Stallion*, a film he greatly admired.

Previous page: The bonding of E.T. and the director.

Eye contact: With eyes modeled on Einstein's, E.T. proved to be both odd-looking and adorable.

Drew Barrymore (Elliott's kid sister, Gertie) takes direction from her real-life godfather. Some 27 years later, she was to direct her own first feature film, *Whip It*.

She was a little dim at first—because, it is said, she was suffering from the "turistas." But she did not remain dim for long. Spielberg said, "It's a story about an alien—a lost boy and a lost alien coming together." He also said, "It was about the divorce of my parents." Still, he strongly felt that the film needed to be kept "as simple as possible, because it is a contemporary fairy tale, after all."

A fairy tale laid out with the simplicity that only the truly sophisticated can sometimes attain. "The alien and the alienated," Spielberg calls the relationship between the wee alien—"lost and alone and three million miles from home"— and Elliott (wonderfully played by Henry Thomas), who is upset by his parents' divorce, uninterested in the kid stuff that had previously consumed him, but not quite ready for the agonies and ecstasies of adolescence. He and E.T. are soul mates—without knowing it, of course.

It is curiosity that at first gets the better of E.T., Spielberg says. "And maybe the other aliens, the botanists, were too busy finding and categorizing the plants they wanted to take home with them." Anyway, he is enchanted with the redwood forest they've landed in, and before he knows it, the spaceship has taken off without him. This brings him eventually to Elliott. And also into peril from the American scientists who want to capture him and study him and, perhaps, kill him with *their* curiosity.

Gertie (left) and Elliott (below, left) say farewell to E.T. The film's themes of reaching out, establishing contact, and finding ways to communicate are exemplified in the iconic poster art (below, right), inspired by Michelangelo.

But not before he and Elliott have bonded. Spielberg has said that E.T.—the first of the many "lost boys" in his movies—is the most profoundly lost of them all.

We sense, without the little guy saying anything about it at all, that he, no less than Elliott, has friends and family—connections—back home, with whom he must strive to reestablish contact.

Yet the film is equally about the theme that first arose in *Close Encounters of the Third Kind,* the need to establish communications between widely—wildly—disparate characters, and civilizations. Says Spielberg: "I think the greatest thing is when people at least make an effort to communicate, reaching out, focusing on the other person, making eye contact with the person they are trying to communicate with, and that person isn't getting it, and when that person doesn't get it, you have to try harder and be resourceful and inventive in trying different ways to get your message across.

"The more people spend time in a locked room, forced to bridge a language barrier, the deeper those souls connect.

A STEVEN SPIELBERG FILM

E.T.
THE EXTRA-TERRESTRIAL

A STEVEN SPIELBERG FILM
E.T. THE EXTRA-TERRESTRIAL
DEE WALLACE · PETER COYOTE · DREW BARRYMORE
HENRY THOMAS AS ELLIOTT
MUSIC BY JOHN WILLIAMS   WRITTEN BY MELISSA MATHISON
PRODUCTION DESIGNER JAMES D. BISSELL
DIRECTOR OF PHOTOGRAPHY ALLEN DAVIAU   EDITED BY CAROL LITTLETON
PRODUCED BY STEVEN SPIELBERG & KATHLEEN KENNEDY

Escorted by his elder brother Michael (Robert MacNaughton) and friends, Elliott snatches E.T. from government agents, who trail in their wake.

Deep friendships are forged when people work hard because they care enough to express to you how they're feeling about something. And that was the bonding of E.T. and Elliott—the two lost souls who absolutely require each other for a very short time, so they can both survive in a spiritual way.

"I mean, for me, *E.T.* is the most spiritual movie I ever made, and that was not an accident. It was something that I always deeply felt."

All of these elements, and more, are present in *E.T.*— they are what ground the film, give it depth and seriousness. But for many in its vast audience (on first release it grossed nearly $360 million in the United States alone, and a figure close to that in the rest of the world), it's likely that they were aware of them only occasionally and possibly subliminally. For the movie is so enchanting on its more obvious levels, starting with E.T. himself—so odd-looking, yet so adorable (Carlo Rambaldi and his team toiled, virtually sleeplessly, for six months to get him right—he had, incidentally, eyes modeled on Einstein's). The little guy was kind of clumsy,

but very bright, and in his slightly awkward way, very loving once he cottons to Elliott, his friends, and family. Whether he's accidentally getting drunk or obsessively building a radio to "phone home," he's a comically earnest figure. Which says nothing of his Reese's Pieces moments (woe be unto the marketing guy at Mars who chose not to allow M&M's candy to be used in the film, thus ceding one of the century's great marketing opportunities to the competing candy of their rival Hershey).

The threats to E.T.'s well-being posed by the American scientists are beautifully orchestrated—genuinely scary, innocence's worthy opponents; the mother's cluelessness and good nature is delicately handled; Elliott's pals' coming to consciousness about E.T.'s meaning in the largest sense is slow-dawning, but finally impassioned.

I think the heroes' escape from their oppressors, with E.T. tucked into Elliott's bike basket as they pedal madly down the street and into the sky for the rendezvous with E.T.'s rescuers from his home planet, is one of the most privileged moments in all of cinema, for which Spielberg

"*E.T.* was a great experience for me because I wanted to be a dad after making it. I wasn't a father and I kind of became a father to those three kids, especially Drew Barrymore, and so that movie sort of changed my life in a very tangible way."

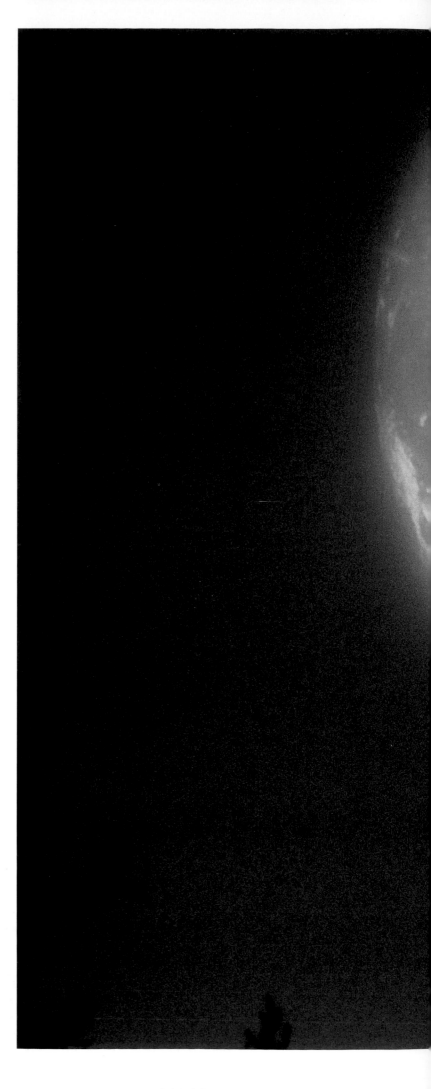

Creating the signature silhouette shot of Elliott and E.T. against the moon (left), at which point the violins in John Williams' unforgettable theme music made them soar (right).

credits John Williams' scoring. "I can make those bicycles lift off. We can do that. But John rewrites my movies musically. John Williams makes them truly airborne, because the audience lifts off the ground on John Williams' violins. And the audience is carried across the moon or the sun with John's string section and his horns later on when they land. I think the last 15 minutes of *E.T.* is close to an opera, because of John Williams' contribution to that movie."

So we soar, as perhaps we have never quite done at the movies, before or since. It is inspirational. And comical. And yet, even as we thrill to the sequence, we feel an odd tickling in our throats. We want E.T. to attain his heart's desire, to at last go home. Yet we are profoundly reluctant to let him go. As was Spielberg. When he was shooting the final farewell sequence it occurred to him to alter the picture's ending—to have E.T. stay on earth, perhaps have the little guy be taken to Wright-Patterson Air Force Base for further investigation, further adventures. But, no, he decided, that was for some other picture.

Spielberg does not cheat on the final farewell to E.T. All the ambiguous emotions of their parting are played in full, though in understatement. And in full knowledge that in that sequence Elliott is becoming a man, prey to the ambiguities of adulthood—its occasional joys, its perhaps more persuasive, more pervasive, sorrows. Will this utterly unique adventure be enough to sustain him during the long lifetime ahead of him? (If this were "real life" he would be only about 40 years old today.) Or will he be living a left-over life? We have to believe that this good kid will have everything in perspective. As Spielberg does—not denying his past triumphs, but always looking ahead.

Still, because of the divorce in his own family, Spielberg admits that "a lot of my films are about the recapturing of the American dream of family. You know, I have that

"For me *E.T.* was both the quintessential story of my childhood and at the same time the end of my childhood, and it gave me the courage, based on its success, to start to tackle more adult subjects. *E.T.* gave me a kind of free pass to fail."

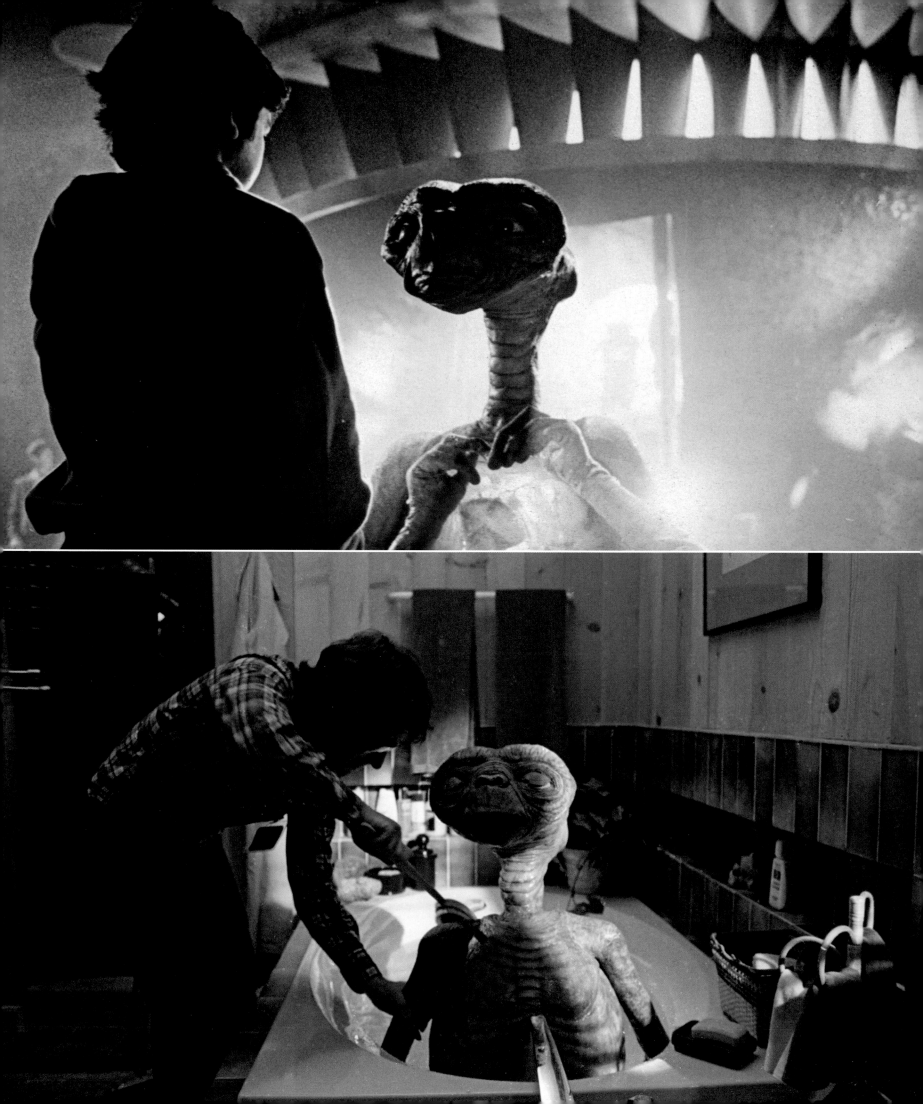

with my family now. I've worked very hard to achieve a nuclear family, but at the expense of understanding what it feels like to come from where your parents separate and divorce."

Here I don't quite follow him. I concede, of course, the contentment of his family life—it is something he alludes to a lot (he still drives his children to school in the morning and he tends, whenever possible, to leave work early to spend time with them). But I think Elliott's situation as the child of divorce haunts Spielberg at least occasionally. As a matter of fact, I think Elliott is a projection of Spielberg, a kid working his way through the difficulties, the sheer absences, of divorce, and eventually coming out on the other side of them, more or less whole, more or less healthy, thanks in his case to what might be called the divine intervention of a distinctly odd, distinctly wise little fellow who never was, but ought to have been.

When the kids are racing to return E.T. to his rescuing ship, they run into some other bikers who wonder what the fuss is about. Elliott explains: "He's a man from space. We're taking him to his spaceship." A dubious interlocutor asks: "Can't he just beam up?" To which Elliott replies

impatiently: "This is reality, Greg." And so it is—for a couple of magical hours.

"My job," says Spielberg, "is to reduce the aesthetic distance between the audience and the experience, so they are lost for two hours and they only wake up when the sunlight hits them in the face as they walk out of the theater. If I can achieve that and they're not thinking about what they have to do tonight and where they have to drop the kids after the movie, in the middle of the movie, then I've succeeded. I think all of us are either successes or failures based on how well we can entrap the audience inside the experience of the story we're telling. And they thank us for it, as opposed to them saying, 'Oh, I wish I hadn't been part of this experience.'"

I guess there must be people who do not respond to *E.T.* There is no movie so bad that it does not have its fans, no movie so good that it does not have its doubters. But in this case, I don't especially want to know any of the latter.

It is perhaps worth noting that, for all its success and acclaim, *E.T.* did not win any major Oscars that year. The big prizes went to *Gandhi*, Richard Attenborough's earnest, deadly dull (and now nearly unwatchable) epic.

Opposite: The final farewell. Elliott declines the invitation to join E.T. (top). Bathed only in soapsuds and not glory, as *E.T.* did not win the big Oscars that year (bottom).

Above: The director resists the temptation to take Elliott's place. "This is reality."

INDIANA JONES

AND THE

TEMPLE OF DOOM

(1984)

"I got separation pangs. I knew that if I didn't direct *Temple*, someone else would. I got a little bit jealous, I got a little bit frustrated."

For reasons not entirely clear—except perhaps to studio executives—Warner Bros. in the early 1980s thought there might be fun and profit to be had from making an anthology movie based on the Rod Serling *Twilight Zone* television series, employing some of the better directors of Spielberg's generation, including John Landis (then coming off the huge commercial success of *Animal House* and *The Blues Brothers* and the cult hit *An American Werewolf in London*) as well as Joe Dante and George Miller, with Spielberg and Landis executive-producing. The thing would be introduced by Dan Aykroyd and Albert Brooks, telling scary *Twilight Zone* stories on a night drive.

Above: The director takes an overview within the mines.

It doesn't sound like much, and it is hard to see what Spielberg saw in the project—other than doing something that honored the nostalgia he felt for the TV shows of his childhood. No one bargained for the terrible accident that occurred on July 23, 1982. Landis was shooting a portion of his film, involving a bigot played by Vic Morrow, who has the tables turned on him when he is transported to Nazi Germany, the Ku Klux Klan South and Vietnam. In the Vietnam section he is pursued by a helicopter. In the event, the detonation of debris-laden special-effects explosions caused damage to the rotor blade of the helicopter, which crashed, killing Morrow and two Asian child extras who were working in the scene with him.

The incident appears to have been the result of pure mischance, but, of course, there were criminal proceedings and suits for damages as well. Spielberg was in no way culpable—he was not on the set that night. Landis and four others were charged with involuntary manslaughter and acquitted of the charge after a lengthy trial. Landis was later admonished for circumventing the State of California's child-labor laws in hiring the two children

killed in the accident and the studio had to settle, out of court, actions pursued by the children's parents and Vic Morrow's children. The studio briefly considered shutting the production down, which would have been the wisest course, but it did not do so. Spielberg, however, chose to do a less edgy story than he was originally scheduled to do. Called "Kick the Can," it was about a group of senior citizens reverting to childhood. He shot it in six days and it was eventually criticized for reverting to some of the sentiments he had previously so successfully advanced in *E.T.*

There was a certain resentment against Spielberg in the critical community at this time. He had proved himself with high adventure and he had proved himself with lovely evocations of childhood. He had enjoyed great financial success—likely the greatest in the history of his medium, certainly for one of his age. The question was, would he ever make a movie exploring sober and mature emotions?

That he now turned to *Indiana Jones and the Temple of Doom* did not augur well for him, especially with the critics. The film has its felicities—notably the best opening sequence of the series. It takes place in a Shanghai

Opposite: With Ke Huy Quan
(Short Round), Indy takes control
of the scene board (top). An elephant
ride too many caused Harrison Ford
back disc problems (bottom).

Above: Time out. Kate Capshaw
(the director's future wife), Spielberg,
George Lucas, and Harrison Ford.

"The prettiest thing that came out of that film was my future wife. And the PG-13 rating, which was invented because of it."

Kate Capshaw was a captivating presence as Willie Scott, a Shanghai nightclub singer. Here shown in consultation with Spielberg (opposite, top); in performance singing "Anything Goes" in Mandarin with a host of dancers (opposite, bottom); and in peril with Short Round (above).

nightclub in 1935 and it involves gangsters, diamonds, poison, antidotes, and a mad scramble for all of these items, plus balloons, and a hair's-breadth escape to an airplane that is scarcely less exciting. I don't think Spielberg ever orchestrated a more intricate and entertaining 15 or 20 minutes than this one. The piece also introduces Indy's traveling companions—a brave, resourceful kid named Short Round (Ke Huy Quan) and the club's singer, Willie Scott, played by Kate Capshaw, who won the role in competition, it is said, with over a hundred other actresses, and who would soon have a much larger role in Spielberg's life. She is the opposite to Karen Allen's rather Hawksian woman in the first Indy movie, in that she is a good-natured gold digger, who is forever falling off elephants and being frightened by snakes and such like—in other words, a klutz, but one who proves her mettle in the trio's adventures.

These are not as stirring as they might bc. This stray thought occurs: The Indy pictures are at their best when Nazis are involved, as they are in the first and third episodes of the series. Their presence as villains seems to concentrate Spielberg's attention—they are like rehearsals for his more serious subsequent involvement with these agents of evil.

Scenes from *Temple of Doom*. Diners at the infamous banquet (top) were presented with delicacies such as baby snakes, giant beetles, eyeball soup, and chilled monkey brains (which were actually made from custard and raspberry sauce).

The success of *Raiders of the Lost Ark* was such that the minimum of explanation was required on the "coming soon" poster for the sequel.

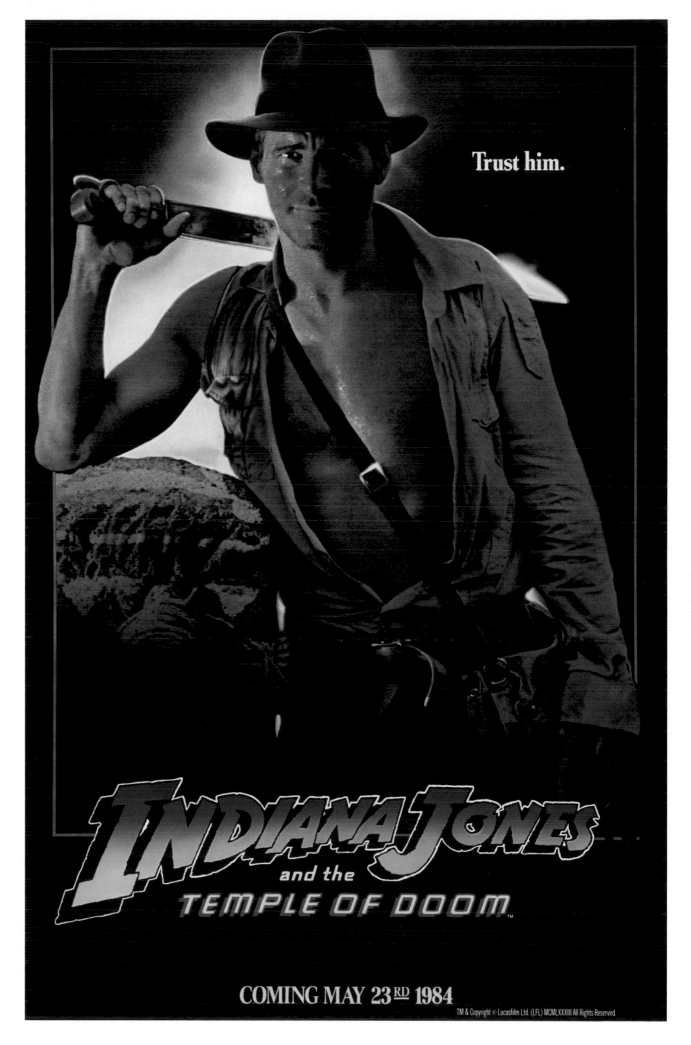

On location in Sri Lanka, the custodians of the Indiana Jones franchise test the rope bridge that features in the film's climactic struggle between Indy and the Thugs.

In *Temple of Doom* he has to make do with purely local opponents. Indy, Short Round, and Willie fall to safety from their airplane (very exciting and highly improbable) and are rescued by the residents of a remote Indian village, all of whose children have been abducted by what turns out to be a Thuggee cult, which has also absconded with a sacred stone, precious to the village. Indy vows to restore the children and the stone. This leads him to a mine and a gathering place for the cult, where the children are enslaved and worked to death. The Thugs capture Willie and Indy and torment them in colorful, unpleasant ways, until, finally, they escape via tram cars that service the mining operations.

It is supposed to be the movie's biggest action sequence and Spielberg milks it for all its worth. Yet it somehow does not quite come off. It is dark and rather cramped in execution—just another chase, if the truth be faced. And one not offering the open-air release of such sequences in the previous Indy film. The movie ends with the children and the sacred stone restored to the village, Willie matured by her harum-scarum adventures and clinching with Indy.

The film did not find much favor with the critics (although it was a box-office success). The more or less standard line on the picture was that it was heavy-handed and witless, not finding room for the humor that had so enlivened its predecessor. It just piled up pretty much non-stop thrill sequences. There was nothing at stake in it that compared to the Lost Ark of the Covenant, which gave the earlier film something that at least passed for weight.

There was a ratings war over the film, with the ratings board insisting that it receive an "R" for its lengthy and colorful violence. This, of course, would have cut it off from its prime, youthful audience. Spielberg called Jack Valenti,

president of the Motion Picture Association of America, and asked him to consider a rating midway between PG and R, and he agreed on the phone. The upshot was the invention of the PG-13 category—which permitted films like this one to be shown to teenagers. Spielberg was all right with that. He had already agreed that children under the age of 10 should not be admitted to the picture. Another three years added to that figure was of small consequence to him.

The larger, indeed incalculable, legacy of the picture resulted from the presence of Kate Capshaw in the cast. She is quite good in the picture, but in time she and Spielberg would fall in love, and marry, and have (or adopt) five children, engaging in one of Hollywood's happiest marriages. Spielberg's contentment with this partnership— he relies heavily on his wife for advice and support—is (no other word for it) inspirational to observe.

At the center of it all, as usual, the director puts his vision into words and actions.

THE COLOR PURPLE

(1985)

"The big difference in *The Color Purple* is that the story is not bigger than the lives of these people. I didn't want to make another movie that dwarfs the characters. But here the characters are the story."

"I don't think I could have made *Schindler's List* or *Empire of the Sun* without *The Color Purple*," claims Spielberg. "That would have been impossible. I didn't have the maturity, the craft, and the emotional information to be able to acquit the Holocaust in an honorable way, without bringing shame to the memory of the survivors and especially to those who didn't survive. Every movie I made before *Color Purple* goes better with the smell of popcorn. *Color Purple* didn't."

In her first role in a major studio production, Whoopi Goldberg's performance as Celie Johnson earned her an Oscar nomination for best actress.

The book was pressed upon Spielberg by Kathleen Kennedy, although Quincy Jones, who composed the film's score, was an important go-between in setting up the project—which almost immediately drew protests from racial-interest groups, who complained particularly about the degradation of the leading black male character and even accused the film of promoting lesbianism. To some degree these doubts were deflected, if never fully stilled, by enlisting the book's Pulitzer Prize-winning author on the film's side. Alice Walker, a shy, almost reclusive woman, met Spielberg and Kennedy, and they allayed many of her doubts about the project. She was to be found on location a good deal of the time, coaching the actors in their turn-of-the-twentieth-century accents and being generally helpful to the production simply by being present at the creation.

The story was a complex one, involving a group of black women variously abused by the men in their lives, but ultimately triumphant over them—or at least able ultimately to find decent lives in difficult circumstances. Central to the story is Celie (Whoopi Goldberg), an abused child and, indeed, an abused woman. What saves her, in the end,

is her strong relationships with three women: Shug Avery (Margaret Avery), blues singer and mistress to Albert (Danny Glover), who is Celie's husband; Celie's younger sister, Nettie (Akosua Busia), who becomes a missionary in Africa; and strong-willed Sofia (Oprah Winfrey), who is eventually beaten and jailed for disrespecting members of the white Southern ruling class.

The picture is also significantly about—well, yes—communication. Throughout the book and film the women constantly struggle to talk with one another, to speak of the things that are closest to their hearts that have the power to transform their lives. This includes lovely scenes in which one woman teaches another to read, there is a hand-clapping game that practically defines a relationship that stretches over almost 40 years, there is even a lesbian relationship, implicit in the film and much more frankly stated in the novel. "I just went for a kiss between the two women," Spielberg says. "I did that because I wasn't ready to do anything more than that."

That decision, of course, assured an audience of millions more than the inevitable "R" rating that anything stronger

Spielberg had a definite tone in mind for *The Color Purple*—"faces, interiors, exteriors, the beauty of the land, à la John Ford. A very hard story inside this beautiful picture frame."

would have invited. But it also assured the picture of a tone more in keeping with the approach he finally settled upon. For some time he "flirted" with the idea of doing the film in black and white, "because I was afraid of myself—afraid I was going to sugarcoat the book. If at least I shot it in black and white there would be no sugar to coat anything with."

In the end, however, he and cinematographer Allen Daviau decided on the opposite approach. They wanted to make the film look beautiful—"faces, interiors, exteriors, the beauty of the land, à la John Ford. A very hard story inside this beautiful picture frame.

"I had a tone in mind—it was going to be moments of sheer horror, but set in a tapestry of purple flowers and beautiful farm land and growing corn."

He admits that this approach "might have overwhelmed the collective memory of what Alice Walker put on paper." Certainly, there were critics who felt that was true. They were intent, at the time, on holding Spielberg to the highest standards on this, his first "serious" film.

He had other concerns as well, not all of them to do with the film. He had been courting the actress Amy Irving and, in 1985, the year of the picture's release, he married her. She was the daughter of the actress Priscilla Pointer, and Jules Irving, who, with a partner, had succeeded Joseph Papp as director of New York's Public Theater. She was,

as well, a strong and promising performer, notably in a pair of Brian De Palma movies. Their marriage was, to say the least, stormy. To make a short story even shorter, it lasted only four years, producing Spielberg's first child, a son, Max, and much fairly well-publicized acrimony. It is not for an outsider to say what went wrong with the match and its principals have not spoken about it. Amy Irving continued with her career, working in film and on the stage. The press reported a huge settlement in her favor, though one has to believe it was surely not as large as some sources claimed.

Spielberg's personal life did not, so far as one can tell, affect his work on *The Color Purple*. He had wanted to do the film, but he was hesitant about it as well. Before production began, he was aware that many in the black community were critical of a white man directing this quintessentially black subject. And he was, as well, aware of his reputation for doing much softer kinds of films. If he were not, there were plenty of people, particularly in the black community, ready to remind him.

The critics reckoned without Spielberg's willfulness—when he has set his course, he will not be deterred—and his directorial skills. The picture is long and it is not without its awkward moments. In some sense, though, these are sources of strength as well. The people of this film, particularly some of the male characters, are not altogether pleasant company.

They make mistakes. They are patronized. They have, indeed, their evil impulses. And they are situated in a time and place that often uses them harshly.

On the other hand, they are strong and determined, without quite knowing where those qualities come from. All they know, really, is that the best among them must keep going forward, looking for the better life—not mostly in any material way—that they instinctively know is promised them. You could say that *The Color Purple* is uplifting, perhaps even sentimental in its way. But not in a particularly overt way. On the whole, Spielberg passed his test: With this film he earned the right to be taken seriously—though some of us thought he had already earned that right with his very expert handling of lighter topics. No one would ever again say that he was incapable of sober topics, soberly handled. It was, in a sense, the picture that began the process of converting him into a more or less total filmmaker.

Above, left: Laurence Fishburne, seen here as Swain, was another actor who counted *The Color Purple* among his early screen appearances and went on to greater fame.

Above, right: Oprah Winfrey (Sofia) hones her interviewing technique. On Spielberg's left is his long-standing producer, Kathleen Kennedy, who urged him to make *The Color Purple*.

EMPIRE OF THE SUN

(1987)

"For the first time, I'm making a movie to satisfy me, not the audience."

A STEVEN SPIELBERG Film

Empire OF THE SUN

To survive in a world at war,
he must find a strength greater
than all the events that surround him.

WARNER BROS. Presents A STEVEN SPIELBERG Film "EMPIRE OF THE SUN" Starring JOHN MALKOVICH
MIRANDA RICHARDSON · NIGEL HAVERS and Introducing CHRISTIAN BALE
Music by JOHN WILLIAMS   Director of Photography ALLEN DAVIAU, A.S.C.   Executive Producer ROBERT SHAPIRO
Produced by STEVEN SPIELBERG · KATHLEEN KENNEDY · FRANK MARSHALL
Screenplay by TOM STOPPARD   Based on the novel by J. G. BALLARD
Directed by STEVEN SPIELBERG

 AMBLIN

DOLBY STEREO
IN SELECTED THEATRES

READ THE
POCKET BOOK

SOUNDTRACK AVAILABLE ON
WARNER BROS. RECORDS, CASSETTES AND CD's

WARNER BROS.
A WARNER COMMUNICATIONS COMPANY
©1987 Warner Bros. Inc. All Rights Reserved
ADVANCE SHEET · PRINTED IN U.S.A.

"Christian was easy. He listened more than he spoke and he invested himself both spiritually and consciously into the character of Jim."

Previous page: The boy reaching to the sky with his toy plane, enchanted by the magic and mystery of flight, is one of the leitmotifs of *Empire of the Sun*.

Below: The director builds the Dickensian relationship between Jim and John Malkovich's character, Basie.

It was David Lean who first stirred Spielberg's interest in *Empire of the Sun*. The protean English director had read J.G. Ballard's autobiographical novel, which had about it an epic quality, and he asked Spielberg to enquire about the film rights, which were controlled by Warner Bros. The studio said that they were already committed to another director, and that appeared to be that. Then, six months later, Terry Semel (the co-leader, with Robert Daly, of Warner Bros.) called, saying that the deal had fallen through, and wondering if Lean was still interested. He was not. But Lean added, according to Spielberg, "You should do it. I think this is right up your alley."

Even at the age of 13, Christian Bale, as one of Spielberg's "lost boys," was already displaying the intensity that would define many of his future film performances.

There was already a version of the script, which had been written by Tom Stoppard, whom Spielberg had not previously known, except by reputation as one of the leading English playwrights of his generation. "I just went absolutely bonkers over Stoppard," he says, "and Kathy Kennedy and myself and Tom Stoppard, as a team, began working on another draft of the screenplay."

It is not hard to trace the sources of his enthusiasm. Jim Graham (played by Christian Bale) is a child of privilege in the pre-war expatriate community of Shanghai and, as Spielberg puts it, an "odd duck." He is, for one thing, obsessed with flight, "the idea of being airborne, free of the earth—just short of dying and going to heaven, being able to fly." That, right there, had an obvious appeal to Spielberg. Shortly after we meet Jim, we find him at a garden party, duded out in a sort of boyish version of a harem outfit, racing through the gathering with a toy plane, making zooming sounds. He also finds a downed airplane, climbs into its cockpit and engages in an imaginary dogfight.

He is indeed, as Spielberg imagines him, "an odd duck." A little boy who talks to God (who does not respond) and even plays tennis with him. His obsession with flight, we realize, has something to do with rising into the sky to attain greater proximity to the Almighty.

Meanwhile the Japanese now occupy Shanghai. And in a sequence that is among Spielberg's best stagings of mass action, Jim and his mother are caught up in riotous scenes of panic on the Bund, Shanghai's main thoroughfare. Jim is holding his mother's hand; in the other he holds his toy airplane, which he drops. He pulls away to retrieve it, and loses her in the crowd. He then returns to his deserted home, where he imagines—or half imagines—sexual encounters of a mysterious and troubling kind.

This was the first Western film to which China had opened its doors for location filming, but in a limited way. The company had just 21 days to shoot in Shanghai, most of which were consumed with the huge Bund sequence. Some of that was easy—the street had not evolved much over the years, so it was pretty much just a matter of changing the signage. Some of it was very difficult—as many as 10,000 extras were required. And they even had to build something like 50 rickshaws for the sequence, as the vehicles had been banned by communist China. Most of the rest of the film was shot in Spain and England, on sound stages and on location. It went somewhat over budget, and there were problems with the weather, but still—at an eventual cost of around $38 million—it was, relatively, a bargain. And it realized, so far as one can tell, all of Spielberg's ambitions.

"One of the things I responded to in the book," Spielberg says, "was the fact that it made selections of what a child grabs on to with his eyes compared to what an adult would see. Kids in their imaginations just create these amazing real-time scenarios that are triggered by what they choose to look at. The book was filled with visual references. And that's what I really responded to, being able to tell this story through the eyes of a child, and to show the child losing all that. It's about the death of childhood. The story is probably quintessentially more about the death of childhood than anything I've made before or since."

This is a process that begins when Jim is captured near his home and taken to an internment camp, where most of the film takes place. More important, he is now officially one of Spielberg's "lost boys"—perhaps the most lost of them all.

But it soon becomes clear that he is a very resourceful one. "I did identify with Jim as a disenfranchised kid, having to fend for himself," Spielberg says. "To pick up skills that he never dreamed of having, of having to ingratiate himself in order to survive. Bang, like that, he's got to figure

"I wanted to draw a parallel story between the death of this boy's innocence and the death of the innocence of the entire world. When that white light goes off in Nagasaki and the boy witnesses the light—whether he really sees it or his mind sees it doesn't matter. Two innocents have come to an end and a heartbroken world has begun."

The set-piece sequence on the Bund in Shanghai, in which Jim (Bale) becomes separated from his mother, was a rare example of a US film crew being allowed to shoot in communist China. They had to move fast, as they were granted only 21 days to complete their work.

Overleaf:
A serendipitous location moment for the filming of the American P-51s bombing the Japanese airbase.

out who he is—a rich, entitled boy who goes from riches to rags in this lost world. That so intrigued me. That's why I made the movie."

The chief instrument of his survival is John Malkovich's Basie. He is the camp's scrounger-in-chief and, really, the master of its secret life, the man who—for a price, of course—makes life bearable—survivable—for its inmates. He is both a darkly comical and occasionally deadly figure in this story. "Malkovich sees in the boy a shadow of his former self. He sees hope in this boy, that he could become a protégé and become a terrific scrounger, like himself. And the boy looks to Malkovich, basically, to provide his next meal, literally as a way to survive, to be part of his clique, to be inside that circle. Basie is Fagin and, in a sense, Jim is Oliver. And they have a Dickensian relationship."

But not quite—at least not on Jim's part. For on the other side of the camp's fence, there is a Japanese airfield, and a pilot who is being trained for a kamikaze mission. He and Jim are in silent contact, almost "a holy communion" as Spielberg puts it, "a beautiful communion having to do

with flight." In a sense, this is the film's saving grace. The Japanese flier keeps alive in Jim his former reverence for flight, the best part of the boy he had been before war came to him.

The war must end, naturally—and, for Jim, in a spectacular way—when American P-51s suddenly appear in the skies above the camp. It was a serendipitous moment for Spielberg. He was on the location early one morning and realized that the moment was utterly right for the sequence. He hastily threw together its elements—and in the event a low-flying pilot spots Jim and acknowledges his presence with a cheerful wave, a sort of welcome back from what was a kind of dream to more ordinary realities.

But not quite. Freed from camp, Jim wanders into one of Spielberg's most impressive sequences. It is a stadium. In it is gathered the detritus of Jim's past life—Biedermeier and Josef Hoffmann furniture, Cheval glassware, and Rolls-Royce and Bentley automobiles, too—the vestiges of a lost empire. And a sight that must have staggered J.G. Ballard when he first beheld it.

"I don't think I've made a dark movie. But it's as dark as I've allowed myself to get, and that was perversely very compelling to me."

"I think I made it larger than it really was," Spielberg says, "because I was trying to make a point. It was the refuse of a society that didn't see the war coming. It didn't see it until it was too late, which is always the case with people who are behind the controls of their own businesses or the economy—they're the last ones to see something coming down the road."

Jim finds his parents at this strange and haunting fair. But, as Spielberg says, "he's not going to stay very long because I end the movie with his eyes closing, and they're the eyes of an old man. He won't spend that much longer at home with his parents and will probably go out on his own, and probably become a novelist, which is what Ballard became in real life."

On release, the film was only moderately well received and probably did no more than break-even business. Over time, however, its reputation has continued to grow. David Thomson, the film historian, now regards it as Spielberg's best work and he is not alone in that opinion. I surely

agree that it is among his finest works. There is an ease and assurance about it—it has a kind of inevitability that is quite astonishing, given the rather knotty tale it unpicks, and given the far-flung nature of the locations that were imposed upon it. And the acting is unimprovable—especially by the young Christian Bale, moving seamlessly from the dreamy to the hustle and scuttle of his prison-camp incarnation. There is something unknown, unknowable in this performance that is emblematic of acting at its mysterious best. The Malkovich character, too, is a fascinating figure—a hard, shrewd man, not at all likable, but with a snake-like fascination to him as well.

Empire of the Sun advances two of Spielberg's major themes—the magic and mystery of flight and the child who is first lost and then finds himself—in an uncommonly graceful way, without resort to compromise or comfortable answers. This, far more than *The Color Purple*, announces Spielberg's arrival as a fully mature filmmaker. For in it he is less beholden to genre conventions. This, truly, is a one-off.

Preparing a scene between Bale and Nigel Havers as Rawlins, the prison-camp doctor—a more wholesome role model than Basie the scrounger-in-chief.

In just four years, Jim has evolved from "an odd duck" of a boy into a war-hardened young adult with "the eyes of an old man."

INDIANA JONES

AND THE

LAST CRUSADE

(1989)

"The Grail legend was interesting to me symbolically because it represented the search for oneself—but making a movie about that seemed too esoteric for this genre."

Who knew that Indiana Jones was another of Spielberg's "lost boys"? But such is the case. For the first time in the series, he has a significant back story, which reveals that Indy's mother has died and that his father, played by Sean Connery, has been absent without leave for much of his childhood. The old man has spent much of his life on a far-flung pursuit of no less than the Holy Grail. On those rare occasions when he is at home there is no occasion when the two talk about anything meaningful—a defect that the father is notably blithe about.

Previous page: The director at work on his favorite of the four Indy films.

Jones *père et fils*, Sean Connery and Harrison Ford, unite in search of the Holy Grail.

The film differs from its predecessors in that the opening action sequence is somewhat more tied to the main story. We find the young Indiana Jones (played by River Phoenix) in a cave, recovering "The Cross of Coronado." This piece belongs in a museum, he keeps repeating, as he eludes, for a long and exciting time, an outlaw band whose aims are wholly mercenary. When, at last, the gang captures the artifact, Indy receives by mail from his father a notebook containing much of the information he has discovered in his pursuit of the Grail.

After a brief transitional sequence, from which, of course, Harrison Ford emerges as the mature Indy, he learns that his father is a captive of the Nazis, so it's off to Venice (and many points east) as the film embraces its destiny as a non-stop action ride. A catacombs sequence full of rats in full squeal, a cruel and pretty girl (Alison Doody) who engages in mildly sado-masochistic sex with Indy (a first for Spielberg), but who turns out to be a Nazi, a boat chase, a trip to a castle from which Indy rescues his father, a trip to Berlin in time for a book-burning, a zeppelin ride, a tank battle in

a North African desert, a trip to a lost city, a descent to an underground cavern where at last the Grail and its faithful ancient guardian reside. And God knows what else.

Denholm Elliott is along for the ride, playing what amounts to a thoughtful, kindly, and somewhat befuddled father figure, but the picture naturally belongs to Ford and Connery, who in the course of their non-stop adventures really do bond, although the elder Jones has the annoying habit of calling Indy "Junior" even in the most stressful moments. Connery gives a wonderfully grumpy, yet always appealing, performance in the role. In his crisp way, he lets Indy know that, although often absent, he has always loved the lad. But he also teaches him an important lesson, which is that men have work to do, obsessions to follow, and that, much as they might occasionally wish it were otherwise, family obligations must take second place to these matters. It is only when, as a more or less mature man, Indy is free to join him as an equal (indeed dominant) partner in their quests that they are able to bond and, in their quarrelsome way, become friends.

Feet up, but eyes down
—and lost in the story.

> ## "I'm making the third movie to apologize for the second. It was too horrific."

River Phoenix, as the young Indy, rides away with the Cross of Coronado.

The Führer (as played by Michael Sheard) stops to sign an autograph. Most of the Nazi uniforms on display in the Berlin book-burning scene were genuine World War II uniforms tracked down by costume designer Anthony Powell for use in the movie.

Opposite: Indy between a rock and several hard places; and making a getaway with his father on a Nazi motorcycle and sidecar (bottom, right).

As it did in the first Indiana Jones movie, the Nazi nemesis seems to bring out the best in Spielberg. These are enemies worthy of him in their way, representatives of absolute evil, rather than mere plot devices. They are often inept, of course, but they are never less than dangerous in their flailing ways. And Spielberg feels free to satirize them. For example—and this is one of the movie's high points— there is the matter of the Nazi rally in Berlin. It is one of Spielberg's masterfully staged big scenes, and at one point a disguised Indy comes face to face with no less than the Führer himself. He has at this point recovered his father's diary, which Hitler then takes and autographs for him.

The Führer is, for the moment, not the most evil man in the world. He is simply a celebrity going about his routine duties. That Spielberg feels free to indulge this goofy moment, while the torches are lit and the books are still burning, says a lot about his confidence, his mastery, at this stage of his career.

Not enough has been said about the most obvious aspect of his career—the sheer range of it. This movie follows hard upon the solemnity and self-consciousness of *The Color Purple* and *Empire of the Sun*. It is only four years and four films prior to *Schindler's List*. Yet his commitment to it

is no less intense than it is to those other films. Of his peers among his friends and contemporaries (Martin Scorsese, Clint Eastwood, et al.), he has ranged perhaps with more ease and grace from the cheerfully goofy to the heartbreaking with no loss of craft or of spirit. This is not to denigrate the achievements of those friends and competitors. But moviemaking, especially at the expensive and expansive level that Spielberg practices it, is never tossed off. It requires passion and single-mindedness.

It is obvious that in recent decades Spielberg has seemed to think more seriously about his choices, approaching directorial projects with more circumspection, committing to and moving away from them for reasons that are not always clear even to himself, sometimes arriving at moments when he is obliged to make two and even three films back to back (an exhausting process that he says he hates).

But with *Indiana Jones and the Last Crusade*, audiences sensed that he was all-in on the project—and joyously so. The reviews almost universally spoke of a return to form after the lackluster *Temple of Doom*, although there were occasional warnings that it was time to hang up the bullwhip. He had no intention of doing so. Anything but.

ALWAYS

(1989)

"Some movies don't take off and there's a thousand reasons why ... It was a good experience for me to make that movie because it was all about human emotions. I have no regret at all."

Richard Dreyfuss returns from a successful firefighting mission. The movie itself didn't receive quite so enthusiastic a welcome.

When he was a teenager, Spielberg showed the movie *A Guy Named Joe* to a young woman he was dating. When it was over he asked her how she liked it. Not much, she said. Why, he asked. Well, she said, it was in black and white. It is perhaps superfluous to add that the relationship did not thereafter prosper. But Spielberg remained loyal to the film, which he eventually re-made (and updated) as *Always* many years later.

Previous page: The director, not for the first time, appeals to a higher power.

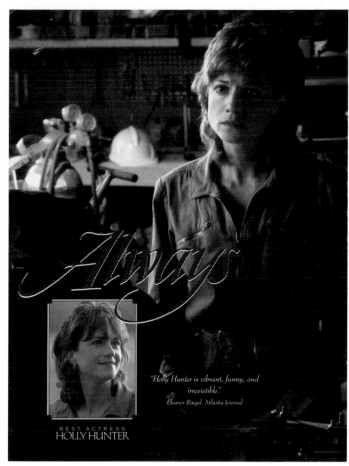

For your consideration: Holly Hunter would have to wait until 1994 to win a Best Actress Oscar—for her role in Jane Campion's *The Piano*.

Opposite (bottom) and above: Boy-meets-girl story—Richard Dreyfuss and Holly Hunter try to strike a spark.

The original movie had been directed by Victor Fleming in 1943, from a script by Dalton Trumbo, and tells the story of a pilot (played by Spencer Tracy) who is killed in action, but hangs about as a ghostly presence. He mentors a young flier (Van Johnson), helplessly watching him fall in love with his former girlfriend (Irene Dunne). He even flies with her on a dangerous mission where she replaces the Johnson character and guides her through it safely. He's something of a wise guy, but because of his posthumous selflessness he achieves peace for himself that, we gather, will extend through all eternity.

A Guy Named Joe is an agreeable fantasy—something of a relief from the more muscular derring-do that dominated wartime screens. It is scarcely, however, a great, forgotten masterpiece. It simply appealed to Spielberg's romantic side, which deserves a few words of explanation. Spielberg's re-make, despite its mystical aspect, is as close as he has ever come to a conventional boy-meets-girl story. It, indeed, traffics in that usual nonsense about the guy being unable to make a "commitment" to the girl and to their love. But, with the best will in the world, Spielberg somehow seems to lack a commitment of his own to their passion. In the event, their love for each other seems rather dispassionate. He says himself that what attracts him romantically is not boys and girls together, but the past,

which he tends to "nostalgize"—whether by re-entering it or by bathing his present-day stories in the light of a few years earlier. (His *E.T.* suburbia, for example, owes slightly more to the world he grew up in than to the 1980s reality it is supposed to reflect.)

In any event, in *Always* the hot pilots of World War II are replaced by the equally hot pilots who fight forest fires in the contemporary American west. (This relocation was the idea of his friend, the director Penny Marshall.) Tracy's original role is reprised by Richard Dreyfuss, Irene Dunne's by Holly Hunter, and Van Johnson's by the ox-like Brad Johnson. The best-friend part is taken by John Goodman and Lionel Barrymore's original wise, if ghostly old guide to the afterlife is prettily played by Audrey Hepburn in what was to prove to be her last film. The film is a quite reasonable adaptation of its predecessor, with Dreyfuss's role somewhat pumped up in accordance with his popularity at the time.

The best parts of the film are the firefighting sequences, which were shot on a no-expense-spared basis in Montana and Washington, with the firefighters' airbase handsomely reconstructed near Libby, Montana. The picture, except possibly in Spielberg's mind, was never meant to be a great film. Its source, with its uneasy blend of whimsy, unlikely romance, and action, was simply not strong enough for that. But it is hard to see why *Always* fell as flat as it did.

I think it had a lot to do with casting. In particular, Dreyfuss and Hunter do not strike any sparks. They mime passion, but they don't particularly live it. He's supposed to be withdrawn, of course—a man who is wedded to his job, especially the life-threatening aspects of it. But he is too cynical and too off-hand in his relationship with her. Not to put too fine a point on it, he treats her as a kind of casual lay, though he sometimes tries to pretend otherwise. Hunter plays a variation on the Hawksian woman, trying to elicit some passion from a man who would much rather have a beer with the boys—when he's not happily flying into danger with them. She tries hard—she really does—but there's nothing at stake in their relationship. John Goodman is un-merry as Dreyfuss's best friend and Brad Johnson stands around stalwartly as his replacement. He has a bit of fun doing a John Wayne impersonation, but you cannot possibly imagine why Hunter would fall for him—except, possibly, because he is as steady and reliable as Dreyfuss is flakey.

There is another problem with the film as well. In wartime America, millions of young Americans were in harm's way. There was a crying need for stories that offered faux reassurance that their deaths would not entirely be in vain, that some kind of happy, improbable and useful afterlife was available to them. That was not the case, realistically speaking, but to this day the majority of Americans believe in angels (according to a 2008 study by Baylor University), so any movie that fed into that fantasy was bound to be welcomed—at least by the more impressionable among us.

But firefighters? Operating in the remoter reaches of our back country? And choosing freely to do so? There's no urgency in that choice. It is, at best, an exotic whim on their part. Glad to have them on board, of course. And good luck to them. But there is no national passion about their fates, no imperative for involvement on the part of the audience. *Always* had to stand or fall as a romantic adventure.

As I've written, romances are not a natural fit for Spielberg. He seems almost shy in this film, unable to muster the requisite passions. That's all right, in its way; he has done better than most when it comes to range and no one is skilled at every possible genre. But this picture never takes flight.

So, despite the skill of its making, it fell flat. The critics were not unkind to it, but the box-office takings were relatively slim. No lasting harm was done to Spielberg's career. It was just a mild misfire—not a disaster like *1941*.

Above: In her final film role, Audrey Hepburn advises Richard Dreyfuss on the workings of the afterlife.

Opposite: Directing even the daisies in the quest for perfection.

HOOK

(1991)

"Every day I came on set,
I thought, 'Is this flying
out of control?'"

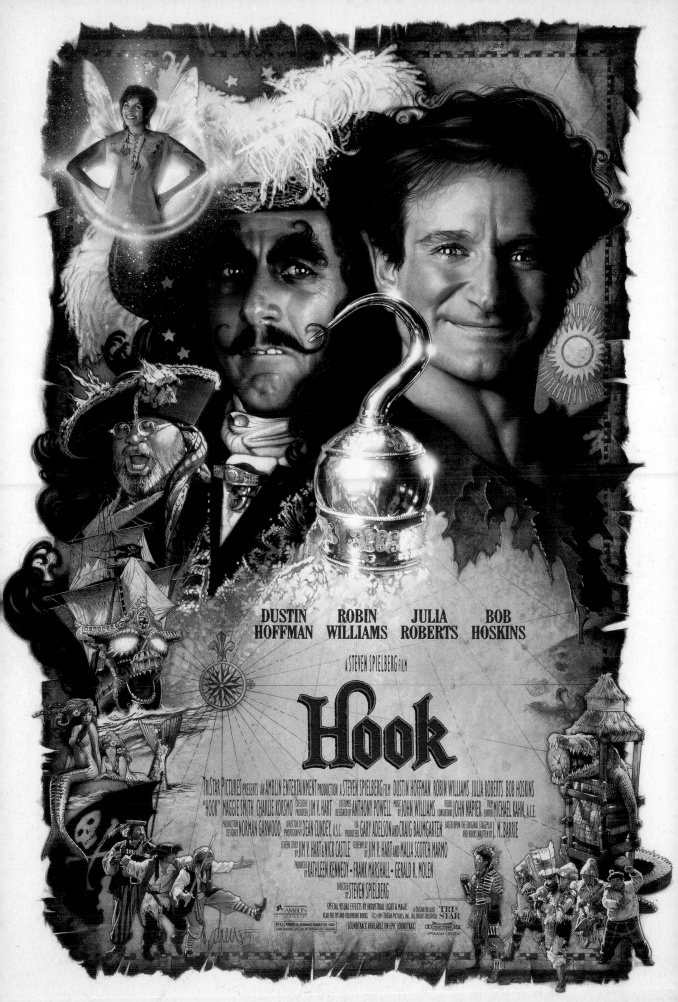

Left: Possibly not the last great adventure with Captain Hook (Dustin Hoffman).

Below: Spielberg's take on Eisenstein's runaway pram sequence.

Opposite: Touched by a divine madness, Robin Williams in full cry as Peter Pan, leading the Lost Boys.

Hook is an anomalous movie in the Spielberg canon, in that, aside from his early work at Universal, it is the only film that did not originate with him. It was in pre-production, with important casting complete, when the announced director, Nick Castle, fell out and Spielberg was approached to take over. It was, of course, a completely logical idea. If ever there were a movie project in which a director and a property seemed made for each other, this version of *Peter Pan* was it.

In the 1980s everyone—including Spielberg himself—thought it was inevitable that someday, somehow, he would make his *Peter Pan* movie and various attempts at doing so were tried. It was the eventual co-screenwriter of the film, James V. Hart, who came up with the winning concept: What if Peter grew up to be an all-American go-getter, who has completely lost touch with his spritely former self? We meet him as Peter Banning (Robin Williams), a mergers and acquisitions lawyer who distractedly loves his children, but mostly sets their needs aside as he pursues ever-greater wealth. My God, he's even afraid to fly.

This conceit was something of a cliché at the time. Many learned commentators were wringing their hands over the American Dad more interested in getting and spending money than he was in getting and spending love on his family. At one point his wife rips his ever-present cell phone from his hand and tosses it out of the window, which deters him from his path only for a moment. It will require the rest of the movie to teach him the error of his ways.

Roughly, it goes this way: Peter and his family visit London, where an aged Wendy (Maggie Smith), the woman who took Peter in and found him his adoptive parents, is about to receive an award for services to orphaned children everywhere. While Peter and his wife attend the ceremony, the villainous Captain Hook (Dustin Hoffman) abducts their

children to Neverland, from which, aided by Tinkerbell (Julia Roberts), Peter must rescue them—in the process learning to fly, have fun, and, of course, put his children first. The picture naturally serves a number of Spielberg's major themes: essentially absent or radically distracted parents; "lost boys" (in this case named as such); and the glorious release of flight, especially after Peter learns to fly.

The script's conceit is serviceable, if not exactly inspired, though far too much time is spent on setting up its rather obvious premises. What really went wrong with the resulting film is more a matter of "production values" than anything else. This was Spielberg tackling a story that was obviously central to his sensibility. No expense would be spared in bringing the film to the screen. And length, too, was no object; this is a self-indulgently long film, around two and a half hours in running time. To the suggestion that the film was over-produced, Spielberg agrees—to an extent.

He says it was "a cousin" to *1941*, without necessarily agreeing that it was a disaster of that magnitude, which, in fact, it was not. No fewer than nine sound stages at the Sony studio in Culver City were employed (it was the first Spielberg film to be made entirely in an artificial setting), the main set consisting of Hook's pirate vessel—35 feet wide, 179 feet long, and 75 feet tall at its main mast. It was by far the largest set Spielberg had ever worked on.

"I'm only not afraid to fly in my dreams and in my movies, but in real life I'm terrified of flying."

These sets, of course, had to be peopled with a vast cast—pirates, children, gawkers—which had to be kept busy at all times. You never saw so many reaction shots.

But some of the film's merriment dies here, in the effort to keep all these people gainfully employed. Spielberg by no means had lost his skill for action scenes, but still, sheer hubbub often replaces meaningful, plot-advancing activity. The film is also surprisingly death-obsessed. More than once Captain Hook refers to death as the last great adventure, something he is rather looking forward to, as he says in his pip-pip accent.

The two leading actors were both friends of Spielberg. Dustin Hoffman tries very hard to give a good performance, pitching his work somewhere between giddiness and menace (more of the former than the latter)—with some surprising literateness thrown in for good measure. This works only intermittently.

Robin Williams is even more problematical. At the time he was touched by a divine madness; an actor who was willing to try anything for a laugh and who, often enough, got one. In performance it sometimes seemed that he was out of control, but he never quite crossed that line. He was, however, increasingly anxious to be liked in more conventional ways. The brakes were being applied —not fully as yet, but still palpably, as in this film. His comedy never soars. He seems to be calculating how far he dares to go and that hurts the film. There is no joy in him when he is Peter Pan in drag.

It seems to me that if *Peter Pan* is to have a chance of working at all it has to dance on air, not deteriorate into food fights (yes, there is a particularly inept one here) and sword fights and entirely uncomical exchanges between Hook and his somewhat heavy-handed second banana, Smee (Bob Hoskins).

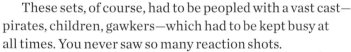

Previous page: *Hook* memorably reprises some of Spielberg's major themes, including the glorious release of flight. It was the first of his movies to be filmed entirely in artificial surroundings over nine sound stages.

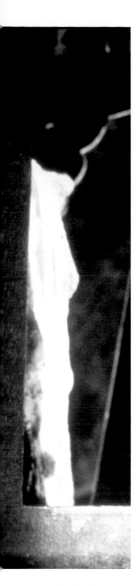

Julia Roberts takes flight as Tinkerbell— "a sweet, light, laughing presence," according to the *New York Times*.

I'm not arguing for an impoverished production, which would be impossible to make in any case. I am arguing for a certain modesty, almost an improvisatory manner—which, at this late date, would have been unattainable for two reasons.

To begin with *Peter Pan* is, by common consent, a "classic." No studio was about to address this property casually. It would have to put its best, spare-no-expense foot forward, lest audiences suspect it was not caring enough. Then there was Spielberg himself to consider. He could not make, at this stage of his career, merely a nice little film. He was almost impelled to grandiosity. In the event the picture almost doubled its budget and its shooting schedule. This is amazing in that it was made exclusively on sound stages, where conditions are, at least in theory, carefully controlled. The weather, for example, is not a factor. Neither are all the vagaries of shooting on location.

It is a handsome, miscalculated film, essentially dead on arrival in the theater. The critics were cautious in their response. They tried their best to find things to like about the movie, but they were also non-committal about it. The picture opened to quite good business—and, indeed, it grossed a profitable $300 million. But it was not a beloved or even entirely likable film, and Spielberg was somewhat chastened. He murmured that this might be the last "big" production he would try, that in the future he would perhaps have to scale back a bit.

As of this moment, he has somewhat come to terms with the movie. His children have taught him to like it, especially (and correctly) the domestic sequences, where Robin Williams is struggling to become an ideal dad. They have a humanity that the more frantic piratical sequences lack. Still, overall, it seems to me a more mechanical, even rather heartless, film than any Spielberg ever made.

JURASSIC PARK

(1993)

"I have no embarrassment in saying that with *Jurassic* I was really just trying to make a good sequel to *Jaws*. On land. It's shameless— I can tell you that now."

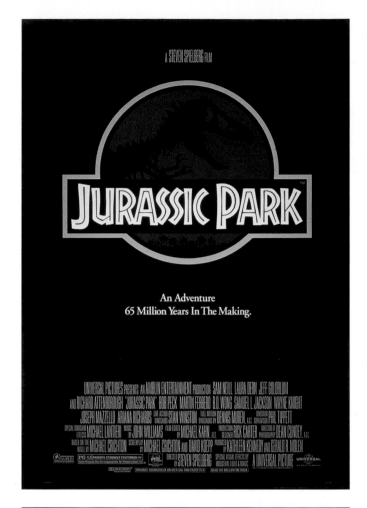

Steven Spielberg had wanted to make a dinosaur movie since he was a child. That ambition increased as he grew older and he became a huge admirer of Ray Harryhausen, the genius of stop-motion animation, the process by which models of prehistoric creatures (or anything else you can think of) are put into motion frame by frame, step by inching step. Spielberg did not particularly want to retreat to the prehistoric past and he could not figure out a way to insert the monsters into a contemporary setting. That was what Michael Crichton did, plausibly enough for Spielberg, in his best-selling novel *Jurassic Park*.

Jurassic Park opened the gates to a new form of digitally created special effects.

Above:
The director directs a director. Spielberg with Richard Attenborough, who plays John Hammond, the owner of Jurassic Park.

Overleaf:
Exit Sam Neill, pursued by Gallimimuses.

His idea, as it was explained in an animated film inserted in the finished film, was that 150 million years ago, a mosquito bites a dinosaur; it then gets trapped in amber, from which you can now extract the DNA from the dinosaur blood in the insect's blood and, lo and behold, you can begin hatching all sorts of very large and mostly baleful creatures from the distant past.

"There was enough credible science that I went, 'That is one of the most genius combinations of science and imagination I have ever witnessed anybody come up with'— and that was all Michael Crichton," Spielberg says today.

Universal bought the movie rights for Spielberg, and he set Crichton and David Koepp to work on the screenplay. It is, appropriately, fairly primitive. It has John Hammond (Richard Attenborough) as the gazillionaire proprietor of a Caribbean island, where he has financed the re-creation of a herd of a half-dozen prehistoric creatures roaming around in beautiful natural habitats for the edification of hoped-for hordes of tourists. He invites two legitimate scientists, Alan Grant (Sam Neill) and Ellie Sattler (Laura Dern), to join and endorse his venture and Ian Malcolm

(Jeff Goldblum), a "chaos" theorist, joins the party to make cynical comments. Hammond's grandchildren are present, too—mostly to be perkily menaced by the rude beasts.

The menacing begins to happen on an orientation tour when, through a combination of bad luck, bad weather, and a bad guy, the T. rexes and their kin escape their compounds and start chomping their way around the island. The movie then settles down to a series of chases, most of which end in narrow escapes. Though dramaturgically primitive, these episodes are directed by Spielberg with his usual élan.

They depend, of course, on the size, athleticism, and sheer mindless ferocity of the creatures, which do not disappoint. Mostly because they are presented through state-of-the-art special effects. Spielberg and his collaborators were standing on the brink of a new movie age—this was "the first movie ever made where the entire success or failure of the story was dependent on these digital characters." He had the artisans at George Lucas's special effects house standing by with more traditional (and, frankly, less realistic) methods of making the monsters move, but he was determined to create digital dinosaurs if at all possible.

"People went to see that movie over and over again because of the dinosaurs, not because the kids had a nice scene where they sat in a tree at night and talked for three minutes."

Two years and something like 60 million dollars were poured into this effort. Which eventually worked a treat.

That, however, discounts the artfulness of the dinosaurs' deployment. Many, if not most, of Spielberg's movies contrive to comment, often wittily, on movie history—a quotation from a famous shot from the past, a reference to a costume or a setting. That's all well and good, but, Spielberg says, "its much more interesting to put a T. rex next to a modern car, or to put raptors inside a modern industrial kitchen or inside a laboratory, things that we today are familiar with, and then you bring the past, 60 million years ago, you bring all of that history into the present and juxtapose a dinosaur with, let's say, a Ford SUV. It's not unlike what Willis O'Brien did with the original *King Kong*.

"I mean, at the beginning of *King Kong*, we're living in King Kong's land. Skull Island is his domain. We're intruders. We're the specimens. So that anything that happens to us, we're fair game. But when they bring King Kong back to New York City, that's where the film gets interesting, because you see King Kong against things

that we take for granted. We no longer take the size of the Empire State Building for granted. It looks a little bit smaller with Kong climbing on it. I think that juxtaposition of the prehistoric past with the contemporary modern world is what made both the book and the movie unique."

Jurassic Park is not—and does not aspire to be—a grand tragedy like *Kong*, which remains after all these years the most heartbreaking of movie spectacles, if only because alone of its breed it is not reliant on literary models for its success. It's a movie original, and the better for it. Not that *Jurassic Park* is to be sneezed at. It does have a strong—perhaps make that breathless—story to tell, and it tells it seamlessly and in a non-stop fashion. And it had the added advantage for Spielberg of pleasing Ray Harryhausen.

They had never met, but one day he was in town and dropped in to meet Spielberg. They naturally hit it off. "He comes over. We have this great conversation. And I say, would you like to see a digital dinosaur? And I brought him over and showed him my first test. Which was the Gallimimuses running across a field. We didn't flesh them. It was just skeletal Gallimimuses running across a field

Reestablishing the reign of the dinosaurs: T. rexes storm the lobby of the main Jurassic Park building (above); flip over a minivan and its terrified occupants (opposite); and disturb Martin Ferrero during a private moment (overleaf).

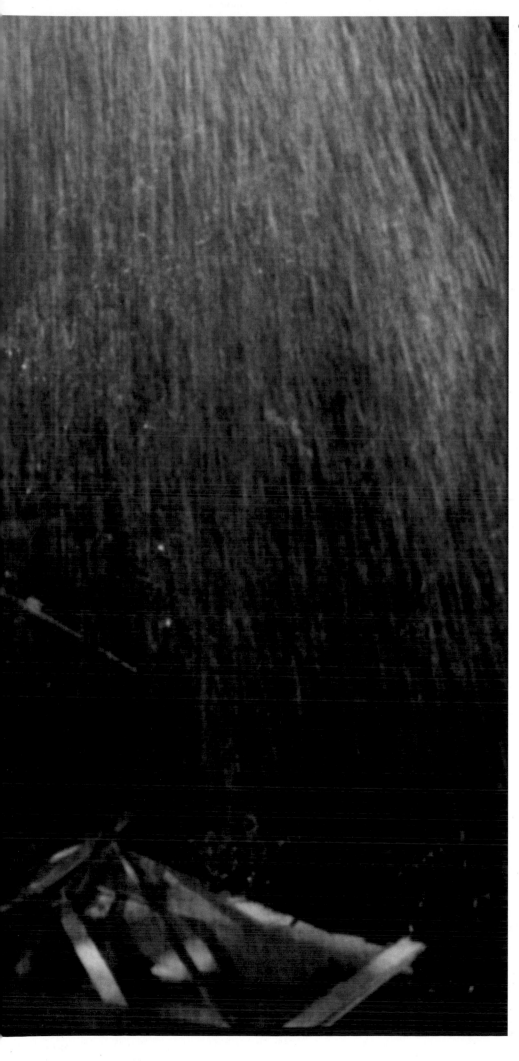

> **"I didn't make it to change the way people saw the world. I made the movie because it was entertaining and it was the kind of movie I wanted to see, which is my motivation for making a lot of my movies ... I'd always wanted to do a dinosaur movie. So this in a sense was my hobby movie."**

and Ray and I looked at this test together. I'd seen the test a week before, and he was the first person I ever showed it to outside of our small unit. He looked at that and he just said, 'Well, there's your future. There is the future.'"

The moviegoing public would soon agree with him. Admittedly, something is lost in this kind of special effects work—the handmade, charming, tireless, slightly awkward quality of Harryhausen's work, which still entrances every new generation of young, somewhat nerdy boys. Set against that, however, is the perfect reality of the work on view in *Jurassic Park*, the sense that these shadows are real, or could be real—and no apologies necessary.

From time to time—it happened with *Kong*, and with *Star Wars*, too—special effects take over the picture they are supposedly serving. They cancel out imperfections of story, banalities of character, the stuff that might sink an ordinary movie. Science-fiction movies are, more often than not, cult successes. Not everyone appreciates the genre. But sometimes they simply override the mass audience's hesitations. People just have to see the damned things.

This happened with *Jurassic Park*. It grossed $200 million in the United States within the first two months of its release, and achieved, ultimately, something like $900 million worldwide. For a time, it would be the highest-grossing movie in history. Even the critics were, on the whole, kind to it. They sensed, correctly, that it represented a seismic shift in the way movies—certain movies anyway—were henceforth going to be made. Now, almost 20 years later, we have doubts about that outcome. The effects are louder and larger, more predictable and pervasive, without necessarily being better. Especially in the summer, the reviewers justly complain about that. They could—although they don't—look back to 1993 and the relative modesty, cleverness—and scariness— of *Jurassic Park*, the movie that started this whole new style of special effects.

SCHINDLER'S LIST

(1993)

"This is the first movie with a message I have ever attempted. It's a very simple message—that something like this should never happen again. But it's one that's very close to my heart."

In the summer of 1982 everyone connected with *E.T.* was "euphoric" (Spielberg's word) with the film's box-office (and critical) reception, so the director awaited with pleasure Sid Sheinberg's Sunday call reporting the preliminary results for the current weekend. They turned out to be excellent, but that was not the main thing on Sheinberg's mind. That morning, he had read a review of Thomas Keneally's novel about Oskar Schindler in the *New York Times* Book Review. "Sir—he always called me Sir—I think you need to tell this story," Spielberg recalls him saying. Forthwith, he sent over the review and the book, and then he optioned the rights.

Previous page: The director in the shadow of Liam Neeson's Academy Award-nominated performance as Oskar Schindler.

Spielberg was more than uncertain about doing it. "I didn't have the maturity, the craft, and the emotional information to be able to acquit the Holocaust in an honorable way, without bringing shame to the memory of the survivors and especially to those who didn't survive."

In essence, he spent the next decade trying to give the book to other directors "who kept giving it back to me."

He doesn't want to mention publicly the names of the directors he pressed the book upon—except one. That was Roman Polanski. Spielberg traveled to Paris to give him the book, which he turned down. "Roman was great. He said, 'You know something? I have a Holocaust story. This isn't the story I want to tell. I don't even know the story I want to tell. I think I may want to tell the story of my life, when I was a little boy in the Krakow ghetto and escaped. I survived the Holocaust. I need to tell my own story.'"

Which, in a sense, he eventually did with a very fine film called *The Pianist*—not autobiographically true, but emotionally very much so.

So Spielberg hesitated over the project for a very long time—the better part of a decade—but with the feeling growing that "it was all meant to come back to me. When something nags at you for 10 years, and like a bad penny keeps coming back, you've got to start taking it seriously.

You've got to start thinking that maybe a few forces are at work that are telling you, 'I may not come back to you again with this. You better say yes this time.'"

Among the forces working on him was the unique way Keneally's book came into being. The author, early for an appointment in Beverly Hills, dropped in to browse in a leather goods shop and fell into conversation with its owner, Leopold Page. In another life, in Poland, he had been known as Poldek Pfefferberg and had been a "Schindler Jew," one of the several hundred Jews who had worked for Oskar Schindler and had been protected by that unlikely man from deportation and death in the concentration camps. Schindler's story was at the time totally unknown, except to those he had saved. After the war he had fallen into poverty and anonymity. Page, however, had papers, contacts, vivid memories. And it was not long before Keneally moved in with him and committed to writing his story.

As for Spielberg, he had his own strong, if obviously second-hand, recollections of the Holocaust. "My mom and dad and my grandparents talked about the Holocaust all the time. They never called it the Holocaust. I never heard that word until I was older. They called it the Great Murders."

As it happened, his grandmother taught English to Hungarian Holocaust survivors in Cincinnati, where the Spielbergs were living when Steven was three or four years

"I was pretty certain that whatever came my way in Poland I could tolerate, and just put my camera between myself and the subject, and protect myself, you know, by creating my own aesthetic distance. And immediately, on the first day of shooting, that broke down."

Spielberg and his new wife Kate Capshaw stand reflectively while on location at Auschwitz-Birkenau (above). The stark surroundings (left), a reminder of the emotionally draining experience of making what was for Spielberg the most important film of his career.

The director issues a flurry of instructions to Neeson.

old, and he learned his numbers based on the numbers tattooed on their arms when they were imprisoned in the camps. He remembers particularly one man who said to him, "I'll do a magic trick for you. You want to see a magic trick?" Of course the child did. So the man would flex his tattooed arm, and lo a six would turn into a nine and vice versa. "I'll never forget that," says Spielberg. "I was a little, little kid—three, four years old. Never forgot that."

Later there was a documentary film—the first film of that type Spielberg ever saw. One day a 16mm projector was wheeled into his class, and a movie called *The Twisted Cross* was run for the students—a study of the Holocaust. "It was the first time I ever saw a dead body on the screen," he remembers. In fact, "I saw piles of dead bodies, stacked like cordwood. I saw a bulldozer pushing bodies into an open trench—all the images that our kids are now familiar with."

These images remained indelible for Spielberg, although it is impossible to say how large a role they played in his decision to, at last, take up *Schindler's List*. Perhaps it is safest to say, as he does, that it was a fated project,

which he finally ceased resisting. A first draft script was written, which didn't appeal to Spielberg. Then the screenwriter Steve Zaillian came on the project. He wrote a "very, very lean first draft," which Spielberg liked, though he felt it needed more heft. "You've got to make the movie longer," Spielberg kept saying. He did not mean by that setting aside Oskar Schindler's story—far from it—but he was beginning to see that more or less the entire Holocaust story, as much as anyone could aspire to tell it, could be encapsulated in this one very rich (and ambiguous) tale. The breakthrough occurred on a location scout in Poland, on which Zaillian accompanied Spielberg.

They went to Auschwitz, and to the other locales of the story, and, on their return, Zaillian went back to the book and "began to expand the story and deepen it in profound ways. He went and he wrote a brilliant, brilliant 185-page screenplay and I shot every page.

"The movie needed to say a lot about the Holocaust, the process of it. The Holocaust was a script that Satan wrote. The whole process of taking away some of your liberties, forcing you to wear a star, forcing a black market inside the Jewish ghetto just for goods to survive, the liquidation of the upper-class Jewish neighborhoods and everybody being ghettoized and then the dissemination of all these people into forced-labor camps or directly to Auschwitz-Birkenau and other death camps for immediate extinction. These were important steps to show the world that there was precision and malice aforethought that led up to the greatest crime in modern history and I couldn't do that in one hour and 52 minutes or a 110-page screenplay."

But yet, Spielberg had to keep his focus on Oskar Schindler, who is one of the great and most enigmatic characters in the history of the movies. As played by Liam Neeson, he is introduced as a feckless fellow, a playboy, casually running an enamel-ware factory in Krakow, but mostly enjoying a life of wine, women, and song—and getting along rather cosily with the Nazi occupiers of Poland. His factory is staffed almost entirely by Jews, however, and he has nothing against them, either. They are good workers and agreeable people, and the practical-minded Schindler is of a live-and-let-live frame of mind. He needs these workers. And, out of that spirit, he acts.

Neeson's performance is a very good and cannily behavioral one. He is a slow and watchful man, his affection for the 1,200 workers he saves growing gradually in an unforced way, his heroism almost unnoticed by him, shown only, for instance, by his delight in a birthday cake his workers present him. There had been a temptation, in early drafts of the script (not by Zaillian), to try to "explain" him in more or less conventional movie hero terms.

That idea, however, was set aside. Schindler, it was decided, must act without explanation. It is this mystery that gives the movie a large portion of its resonance. We are constantly wondering what grace has taken hold

Above: Schindler gives nothing away as one of the great and most enigmatic characters in the history of the movies.

Left: A formal portrait of Spielberg with, from left to right, Ralph Fiennes (Amon Goeth), Ben Kingsley (Itzhak Stern), and Liam Neeson (Oskar Schindler).

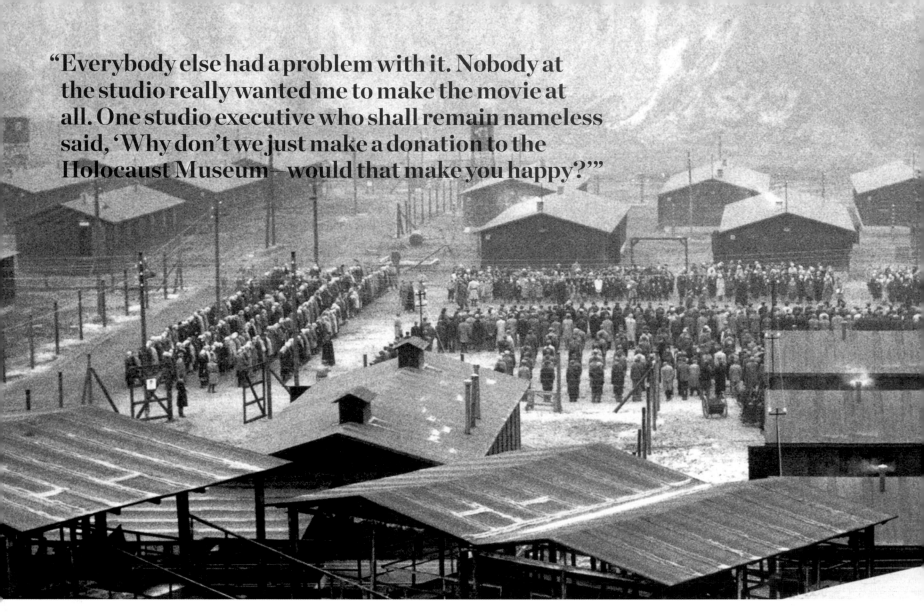

"Everybody else had a problem with it. Nobody at the studio really wanted me to make the movie at all. One studio executive who shall remain nameless said, 'Why don't we just make a donation to the Holocaust Museum — would that make you happy?'"

of this unpromising man, constantly wondering if its grip will suddenly weaken, perhaps plunging him back into darkness and opportunism. It is rare for any movie to have so persistent an enigma at its heart, and that enigma is its unyielding strength.

Zaillian spoke, at the time, of the film having a "Rosebud" quality. That is to say, just as the sled of that name in *Citizen Kane* had a central importance in the formation of Kane's character, so something similar was key to the formation of Schindler's character, though no one could say, with certainty, what that character was. In *Schindler's List*, Oskar Schindler defines himself existentially, acting entirely out of unthought impulse. All we really know about him is that he is in love with the art of the deal (though he was not a notably successful businessman either in the prewar or postwar eras). But in the war years he was touched with a kind of genius. Did he need to deal with the psychopathic Amon Goeth (an unimprovable Ralph Fiennes), commandant of the nearby forced-labor camp at Plaszow? Well, then, he would do so, without once revealing

his loathing for the man. Did he need the friendship of Itzhak Stern (Ben Kingsley), the bookkeeperish custodian of his lists? Well, then, he would have it.

And more. There was a real Itzhak Stern, though he was not heavily featured in Keneally's book. But he was, in Spielberg's view, Schindler's "genius." "He was the man behind the organization of the factory, the one who decided which of the Jews were going to come from Goeth's camp to the relative haven of the Emalia factory. He's sort of the genius in hiding. He keeps to his lists, his numbers, his accounting. But he's the conscience of Oskar Schindler."

But he also "gives to Oskar Schindler something Oskar's never had before, which is an honest friendship. He's never had an honest friendship with a woman, he never had an honest friendship with anybody in the Nazi party, but with this Jew he had an honest friendship."

If there is a moment in the picture when Schindler comes close to acting with self-conscious conscientiousness it comes in the famous scene where he is out riding with his girlfriend. They pause on a hilltop (the scene was made

The psychopathic Goeth prepares to shoot prisoners from a balcony in Plaszow labor camp, near Krakow. The camp was recreated in a quarry for the movie.

precisely where it happened in real life) and glance down to witness the elimination of the Krakow ghetto.

"He watched for a long time," recounts Spielberg. "He saw the little girl in a red coat and he wondered why the Nazis were rounding up and shooting anybody who resisted except the most obvious person, wearing the loudest coat, who was crying out to be captured and put into a truck, why the Nazis were gathering everybody else but this little bright spot, moving down the street—Schindler wondered why something so obvious wasn't being grabbed and put into a truck."

The film was shot entirely in black and white with the exception of a flickering candle at the beginning—and the little girl in her bright red coat. His critics pounced. Here was Spielberg's sentimentalism willing itself out in this, his most austere movie. But that was not his point at all. "I did it in color for another reason, which was that the Holocaust was known about in very small secret circles— certainly Roosevelt and Eisenhower knew." Even the screenwriter Ben Hecht knew; he was putting on pageants

about it all over the United States, in defiance, among others, of the nation's leading Jews, who were in on the secret, too.

Spielberg does not mention the fact that at the upper level of government, and of the American Jewish establishment, the idea of saving or at least improving the conditions of European Jewry was not judged to be an acceptable war aim for the United States. The country was at the time persistently, though not in most instances viciously, anti-Semitic. But still ... it would not do to wage war on behalf of these far-away Jews. To take one small example, during the war years only three fairly minor American films even alluded to them. Most American movies dealing with the underground in Europe—and there were plenty of them—concerned themselves with the plight of "dissidents" fighting Nazi tyranny. These were presented as deracinated idealists since, as a practical matter, many of them were communists, a fact that went conveniently unmentioned as well.

Spielberg: "It was as obvious as a little girl wearing a red coat, walking down the street, and yet nothing was

161

done to bomb the German rail lines. Nothing was done to wipe out the crematoria. Nothing was being done to slow down the industrialized progress of the annihilation of European Jewry. So that was my message in letting that scene be in color."

Spielberg is normally a calm conversationalist. But here his voice rises in intensity. He wants it known that this was not a casual choice, that this scene is, in fact, the essence of his movie. Which was not, he stresses, a technically difficult picture to make. It was, however, "the most emotionally difficult movie I've ever had to make."

What saved him for sanity was the company of Kate Capshaw—his new wife—and some of their children. Their presence in Poland was vital to Spielberg's mental well-being, particularly since he was attending, by remote control, to a full schedule of post-production chores on *Jurassic Park* as well. "Without them, I don't know what I would have done. I'm not sure I wouldn't have been on a sedative or something while I was making the movie."

They "rescued" me, he says. "I mean it may sound melodramatic, I hear myself sounding melodramatic when I say that, but it wasn't that way at all. You know, I had somebody to come home to. Somebody to ground me." Kate and her eldest daughter, Jessica, "were the rocks in my life at the time."

The picture was shot in 75 days on a relatively modest $23 million budget, especially low when you consider that the film's final running time is over three hours. There is no need, perhaps, to consider its astonishing success when it was released in December 1993. The awards—it won Oscars for best film and director and many other prizes. The grosses. The critical acclaim. All of which was richly deserved. Indeed, there seems to me, in the few dissident reviews, a nit-picking quality, something akin to not wanting Spielberg to grow up, to take his place at the movie's highest table, though, of course, he already had.

For Spielberg, though, the afterlife of the movie looms larger than the recognition it achieved. It led to the establishment of the Shoah Foundation, which has, to date, collected some 52,000 video-taped remembrances of Holocaust survivors, which are disseminated all around the world to educational institutions. "It's the only time I've made a movie where something better than the movie came along. *Schindler's List* got a door opened in letting people look at the Holocaust maybe for the first time. I've always looked at it, in hindsight, in retrospect, this way: It was made so the Shoah Foundation could exist. In that respect, *Schindler's List* is the most important film I've ever made and the Shoah Foundation, outside my family, is the most important work I've ever done in the community."

For Spielberg this scene was the essence of the movie—the failure of the Nazis to capture the girl in the red coat (Oliwia Dabrowska) mirrored the failure of the Allies to intervene in the extermination of European Jews.

"For a lot of the survivors who dared to see *Schindler's List*, it unlocked a lot in them. They didn't tell their children and grandchildren any more about what they had been hiding from, about what they went through in the Holocaust. But they did say, 'If you see *Schindler's List*, it's not as bad as what happened to me, but it will give you a very small idea what I went through.'"

THE LOST WORLD: JURASSIC PARK

(1997)

"One of the toughest things about a sequel is the expectation that goes along with it, that you're gonna top the first one. And therein lies all of my anxiety ... you can't really top yourself. You just tell a different story and hope the new MacGuffin is as compelling as the last MacGuffin."

Left: After a break from directing, Spielberg relished getting back on set and in front of a story board.

Below: Shooting the memorable (and arguably deserved) demise of evil Dieter Stark (Peter Stormare). The mercenary is ravaged by a swarm of "Compies," which devour every scrap of him except for his pants.

They're back—some of them anyway: Jeff Goldblum raised from supporting role to lead; Richard Attenborough in a sort of bookend cameo; and, naturally, the dinosaurs. There are more species of them skittering and thumping around in menacing fashion. The special effects folks insisted they were more "realistic" in their—I don't know—"plasticity," and I'm not going to argue with them. Julianne Moore is the principal addition to the festivities.

Previous page: Four years on from *Jurassic Park*, and 22 years from *Jaws*, the director is exposed once again to jagged teeth.

"**The first couple of days on *The Lost World* I was fairly rusty. But like getting back on a bicycle, you pick it up pretty quickly. And then the ambrosia takes over and you kick yourself for not having directed for three years.**"

A scientist, and girlfriend to Goldblum, Moore's character is studying the possibility that the prehistoric creatures have an unsuspected nurturing side, which they occasionally exhibit in their bumbling way. Also along for the ride is the Goldblum character's daughter, alternately scared witless and displaying grit and resourcefulness when the going gets tough.

It turns out that there was a second island, serving as a breeding ground for the creatures, which were then transported to the showplace island of the first film. It also turns out that this second island is known to others besides the beneficent observers we are encouraged to identify with. These others are a small army of mercenaries, led by Pete Postlethwaite, who have been contracted to transport the dinosaurs back to the civilized world where they can be exhibited for profit. This gives *The Lost World* some acceptable antagonists and essentially turns it into an action-adventure film, rather like the first one in the series.

Above: The filmmakers found their Lost World in breathtaking locations in New Zealand and Kaua'i, Hawaii.

Overleaf: For the sequel to *Jurassic Park*, Spielberg takes some of the dinosaurs off the island and into suburban America—including this distressed T. rex (right-hand page) on the rampage in San Diego looking for its kidnapped offspring.

"The first movie was really about the failure of technology and the success of nature. This movie is much more about the failure of people to find restraint within themselves, and the failure of morality to protect these animals."

It certainly is a film where the excitement comes non-stop. And not a bad one, all things considered—Spielberg has not lost his skill in staging inventively detailed, marvelously strung-out action sequences. It's just that the critics of the time thought that after *Schindler's List* he had indeed put aside such childish things.

That, however, was asking too much of him. It is essential to the upkeep of his talent to revel in the meaningless complexities of the cliffhanger—in this case literally so, since the central sequence of the film has Goldblum and Moore trapped in a trailer that one of the creatures is intent on pushing over—well, yes—a cliff. I think Spielberg has to do films like this just to show that he still can. It is akin to the problem D.W. Griffith confronted in the early days of the movies, when, having proved his ability to make "serious" films, he wanted to revert to melodrama of a fairly gaudy sort. These people are, among other things, showmen; they need to stay in touch with their roots and I think it's feckless for people to insist on them doing otherwise. Why would anyone deny them their fun?

Another factor was operating here, too. Spielberg wanted to show a dinosaur stomping around in suburban America—San Diego, to be specific. No problem. Postlethwaite and

friends had succeeded in capturing one of the big tuskers, and was bringing it home for display. It's on a boat. It takes control of the boat, rams into a dock, and is soon looking for its lost child in all the wrong places, scaring the bejesus out of all and sundry. An example of Spielberg's inventiveness: There's one of those big balls by which 76 advertises its presence at gas stations. The dino rips it loose from its moorings and it goes bouncing merrily down the street. What's nifty about this short sequence is that the director throws it away. It's just part of the general mayhem the beast is creating in befuddled San Diego.

Naturally, peace is restored—tranquilizing darts are useful here. No one is going to argue that *Lost World* is one of Spielberg's major movies. But in the longer run of history it's not to be dismissed, either. It leads us on a fairly entertaining chase and its set pieces are as skillful as any Spielberg has ever mounted. We should note, however, that he would very rarely pass this way again. He would make other thrillers. But practically all of them would have some more substance than this picture, something that would at least nominally, occasionally, placate the desire of his critics for him to act like a grown-up for God's sake. As his next film would definitively prove.

AMISTAD

(1997)

"I kind of dried it out
and it became too much
of a history lesson."

"It shares a place in my heart with *The Color Purple*," says Spielberg of *Amistad*. This is not simply because it is also about black people, not solely because it is about people who are enslaved, formally or not, not even because it is also about the difficulty of establishing communications between whites and blacks who, in the case of *Amistad*, share not a single word of common language—though that, finally, is the film's most important theme, aside, of course, from the burning and universal need for freedom.

Previous page and above: Prison bars and slave chains are dominant images in *Amistad*.

In a movie about the triumph of language, the director makes sure he gets his message across.

175

Djimon Hounsou (Cinquè) on the *Amistad*, with mutiny in mind.

Interestingly, the film has its roots in Spielberg's childhood—not the story, of course, but the attitude he brings to it. He was, naturally, subject to anti-Semitism, of a mild, but rather persistent sort. There were never enough Jews at his various stopping points for it to be a large issue and there were virtually no blacks, either. But there were many Native Americans in his school and he was made painfully aware of the racial prejudice that was visited on them. He could not understand this. The Spielberg family was not party to this kind of discrimination. They conducted their lives in good nature, on a live-and-let-live basis. And their only son did, too. He did not understand prejudice then, and he surely does not understand it now. But it is interesting that he raises the subject now, when he is discussing *Amistad*. It is perhaps because it is in so many ways such an unlikely story for him, for any moviemaker— something, quite frankly, that you have to go out of your way to make, even if you are Steven Spielberg. Which is why, of course, he is so proud of having done so.

The film is based on a true incident. In 1839 the *Amistad*, a slave ship bound from Africa to Cuba, is taken over by its cargo, led by Cinquè (Djimon Hounsou), in a bloody revolt. The mutineers order its two surviving sailors to turn around and head back to Africa. Instead, the sailors steer them to America, and eventual captivity there— and king-sized jurisdictional wrangles about whose laws should determine their fate. The *Amistad* flies the Spanish flag. Cuba has papers indicating the slaves are its property. British sailors claim rights of salvage. But the slaves, who cannot understand any of the arguments about their fate, are indisputably on American soil, so perhaps their rights are paramount in these courts. It is, incidentally, good that they cannot understand the proceedings, so casual and patronizing and cruel is the language of the lawyers representing those who would put them back in chains.

Supporting the slaves is a group of abolitionists (Morgan Freeman, Matthew McConaughey, et al.) who argue their case all the way up to the Supreme Court, where John Quincy Adams (Anthony Hopkins), the former President of the United States, and now a sleepy member of the House of Representatives, playing his role just this side of perhaps *faux* senility, movingly (and winningly) states their case.

Morgan Freeman as Theodore Joadson, a freed slave who has gone on to make his fortune in shipping. A leading abolitionist, Joadson lobbies John Quincy Adams on the slaves' behalf.

The picture is dark, static, and, God knows, it is cacophonously talky. Yet it is also, in its unique way, very good. I doubt that anyone but Spielberg could have got such a commercially unpromising film made. It is his theme of the need to communicate writ as large and as dark as it ever was.

Start simply with the fact that he insisted that everyone speak in their languages, introducing the need for hated subtitles throughout—or, if not subtitles, then tedious interpreting. Perversely—or perhaps not so perversely—Spielberg thought this was an advantage, based somewhat on personal experience. "You know," he says, "I find doing interviews in Europe exciting, more exciting than interviews in America, in English, because I get a chance to think while the interpreter is telling the interviewer what I've just said in her language and vice versa.

"I get a chance to look at the person when we're not actively engaged in conversation, processing what I've said, and they get a chance to watch me processing what they've said back to me. I think in a movie audiences love when everything slows down and you can't wait to hear what the interpreter has to say. There's 17 seconds of mystery. It excites the audience.

"It's the reason that courtroom dramas are so provocative and successful—because it's question and answer, question and answer. It sets us up to receive an interesting answer, or to be baffled by the answer. I think it's when someone's interpreting in another language what you have to say, where two people don't quite understand each other and what their lives are all about and then suddenly they understand what they mean to each other, that, suddenly, the audience has these epiphanies that often go unheralded. But they give the audience a chance to say 'I'm part of this story—thank you, you've included me in your story.'"

It does not particularly help the film as a courtroom drama that it is a period piece—dim light, odd costumes, and archaic language. These features have a distancing effect—until they don't and we settle into the conventions of the time. And come to realize that the film is aiming toward an emotional climax that cancels out its maddening Tower of Babel mode.

This occurs with John Quincy Adams' long, beautifully sustained speech to the Supreme Court. After all the misunderstandings, all the failures to communicate (some of them quite willful), here comes this shrewd old man speaking artfully in the American vernacular, part folksy, part self-deprecating, part elevated, and highly principled. Adams is aware that the *Amistad* case is part of the run up to civil war, which is just a couple of decades away, and—Adams, astonishingly, says—a welcome prospect if that is the only way to eradicate the stain of slavery from American society. Here, finally, is the triumph of language in a movie that is mostly about its failures. In its way it is a long-awaited triumph of the American rhetorical tradition. The more welcome for its casual elegance. And for its restatement of the great Spielbergian theme: We must learn to speak our minds with accuracy and eloquence or democracy is doomed. And with it the hope of speaking reasonably to one another of many other things as well.

There is another sequence in the film that is scarcely less good, though in an entirely different way. All along we have not seen what has driven the slaves to their desperate rebellion. It has been hinted at in dialogue, of course, but we have not seen the horrors of the so-called "Middle Passage." Then, suddenly, almost out of nowhere, quite late in the film, we are plunged into it—the floggings, the suicides, the inhumanly crowded conditions, the tossing over the side of dozens of human beings when there is not enough of even the filthy food to sustain them. It is a sequence so horrific and so sustained as to bear comparison to anything Spielberg approached in, say, *Schindler's List*. It shocks one out of the complacency that occasionally threatens this talkative movie.

The film's ending is not an altogether happy one— no triumph of the human spirit here. Cinquè and the rest of the mutineers are set free and sent back to their homes in Africa. He cannot find his family and the movie speculates that they, too, have been sold into slavery. Cinquè himself simply disappears into the vastness of the Dark Continent, never to be seen again. Yes, a slave prison-fortress in Sierra Leone, central to the hideous enterprise, is blown up by a British man-of-war, which gives the film a resounding climax. But we all know that it will require a civil war and more than a hundred years of painful reconciliation— by no means ended today—to heal the scars left by the *Amistad* incident and hundreds like it.

This is a sometimes awkward movie, not at all slickly polished. Spielberg surely knew that it did not have the elements of commercial success about it (in the end it did no more than break even on a budget that was quite modest, perhaps $40 million). It is not often mentioned when people are recounting his career. But it is among the most painful and serious films he has ever made.

"I certainly thought I could withstand any image that I put up on the screen, even images from history, but sometimes they're hard to look at, and especially hard to look at when they're being performed live right in front of you."

Opposite: Spielberg in conversation with Anthony Hopkins, who, as former President, John Quincy Adams, delivers the most memorable speech of a film that is not short on dialogue (top). Final preparations with Matthew McConaughey, who plays the abolitionist Roger Sherman Baldwin (bottom).

Above: Eventually set free, the slaves return to Africa. Unusually for a Spielberg film, this is no triumph of the human spirit.

SAVING PRIVATE RYAN

(1998)

"*Saving Private Ryan* was a tribute to my dad, this was a hundred percent for my dad. When I got the Oscar I said, 'Dad, this is for you. This is yours.' I told my dad many, many years ago that I was going to make a World War II movie for him."

"It's the best, the best experience I've ever had working with an actor. I can say that categorically, the best experience I've ever had."

"I feel so guilty that I'm having so much fun." Giving direction to Tom Hanks as Captain Miller (below); and addressing the troops on Omaha Beach (opposite).

"It was the only time in the several decades of having an agent that an agent actually gave me a screenplay that I wound up directing," Spielberg says with a laugh. Robert Rodat's first draft had, he thought, a few problems, but still he had been looking for years to make a World War II combat film, reading books, stories, screenplays, and watching movies, of course, and this came closest to the ideal he had in mind. "When I read the script I said, 'This is the one.'" As it happened, the script had been sent to Tom Hanks at the same time. "I read the script and he read the script and we, on the telephone, said, let's do this together. So it happened in one day."

Previous page:
Brothers in arms.
The iconic poster art.

The movie was made over many months, which were not, from Spielberg's viewpoint, arduous. Physically, of course, they were. But emotionally, he found himself enjoying the work. That's partly because the film was meant as a self-conscious tribute to his father's generation, aka Tom Brokaw's "greatest" generation. Arnold Spielberg was a trifle grumpy about that. "But Steve," the elder Spielberg said, "You didn't tell my story. What about the 490th bomb squadron? What about those who flew the hump, my friends who were lost flying the hump?" To which Spielberg replied, "'Dad, you're right, I didn't tell that story, but this is for your generation.' I truly was motivated to tell the story for my dad."

It was, essentially, a very simple story. There were, in this war, as in every war, a few families who contributed all of their sons (sometimes as many as four or five) to the uniformed services—the Sullivan brothers, the Niland brothers—raising the possibility that all of them might be killed in action, as, indeed, happened to the Sullivans. In the film, Hanks, as Captain Miller, is in command of a nine-man detachment assigned to locate the last surviving Ryan son and bring him to safety. This is high-priority work; no less than the Chief of Staff, George Marshall, has taken an interest in the matter—and even reads as inspiration a letter written by Abraham Lincoln, who was faced with a similar problem involving a Civil War soldier named Bixby.

Their mission does not present itself, at least at first, as particularly dangerous. It even has its larky aspects, in that for a brief time they are operating on their own, free of orders from those higher up the chain of command. That said, the film's effectiveness utterly depends on the authenticity of its combat sequences, particularly D-Day on the Normandy beachhead, which begins the work, and a fictional firefight, which concludes it—and on the performance of Hanks.

"I think most families would like their boys to grow up to become Tom Hanks," Spielberg says. "I think that's a silent aspiration throughout America, maybe the rest of the world." If there is any actor that could be compared to him, Spielberg thinks it might be Jimmy Stewart. In portraying Captain Miller, "He's strong, but he's simple—a great leader, but a compassionate one."

And one who has his secrets, including the most basic one—what he did in civilian life (he was a schoolteacher, it is eventually revealed). But the main thing about Captain Miller is that he is as frightened as the next man in the hell of combat, but he keeps pressing forward. His performance is a hymn to American dutifulness, but dutifulness without any obvious heroism.

"I wanted the audience to feel the same as those green recruits that were just off those Higgins boats and had never seen combat before, and 95 percent of them hadn't. It was complete chaos and I was trying to put chaos up on the screen."

The set of the fictional ruined town of Ramelle seen from above.

Previous page: Stills from the horrific depiction of the beach landing, which occupies the first 25 minutes of the movie—"so intense it turns your body into a single tube of clenched muscle," according to the *Washington Post*.

The terms and conditions under which Miller operates are set in the opening 25 minutes or so of the movie—the D-Day landing in Normandy in June 1944. I believe it to be the greatest combat sequence in the history of the movies—rivaled perhaps only by the battle that concludes the film (of which more later). The fear and horror of it rendered so intimately and unblinkingly refutes the notion that Spielberg is essentially a sentimentalist.

Yet it is, technically, an atypical sequence for him. "I did the whole thing as stream of consciousness. I had no story boards, no pre-visualization. I did the whole thing from up here [tapping his head], being informed by all the literature I had read about what it was like to survive that day on Dog Green, Omaha Beach." What he didn't know was that it would require 24 days to shoot. People would come up to him and ask what they were going to do next week, and he couldn't answer. "I've just gotten to the sea wall, I haven't gotten up the Vierville Draw yet. The whole thing was being improvised in a very safe, rational, controlled way, but improvised nonetheless. I didn't know what was going to happen next, just like real combat."

After that shattering set piece—which raised the same question the first few minutes of *Raiders* did: Could the rest of the film live up to it?—the picture settles down to the search for Private Ryan. There is comedy, tragedy,

From left to right: Adam Goldberg, Jeremy Davies, Tom Hanks, Matt Damon, Giovanni Ribisi, and Tom Sizemore.

false leads—all the stuff of small-unit combat movies since the 1920s. Especially effective is the way Captain Miller to some degree unburdens himself to Tom Sizemore's Sergeant Horvath. As Spielberg says, he is to Miller what Itzhak Stern was to Oskar Schindler: a mentor, a sounding board, someone he could confide in about what's eating away at him—the body count, the letters home, the collecting of dog-tags. "He needs someone to talk to," Spielberg says. Otherwise his mystery—an important element in his character—will deepen too far to enlist our sympathy.

The rest of Miller's little detachment are standard-issue movie GIs—the Jew, the Italian, and so on. That was a conscious decision on the filmmakers' part. "You can't have seen as many World War II movies as I've seen and not have some of that rub off on *Saving Private Ryan*. It would be impossible for the DNA of all the war movies from time immemorial, Hollywood-style, not to rub off on it." So among other things the movie becomes a kind of commentary on the conventions of the genre, and that is far from a defect, in my opinion. To have done otherwise would have been a kind of betrayal of the pseudo-history from which the film draws so much of its strength. We are trapped in history—even humble movie history—when we try to dramatize our shared past.

In an authentic skirmish, dodging enemy fire.

Tom Hanks's dignified performance as Captain Miller earned him an Oscar nomination. Here in a rare moment of repose (left); in a bunker alongside Private Ryan, played by Matt Damon (opposite, left); and preparing for his death scene (opposite, right).

History is at issue when we compare the combat sequences that begin and end the film. The D-Day landing has the advantage in the sense that it is a fictional account of one of the great passages of arms in American history. You cannot funk it (and Spielberg, of course, does not). It has a truly epic scale and, perhaps more important, its issues are straightforward. The troops must secure the beachhead or be pushed back into the sea, and face unambiguous defeat.

The issues in the fictional battle in the small town of Ramelle at the end are more complex, as is the confusing nature of the conflict—which is hand-to-hand, without a clear design. You don't know, until the very end, who's winning and who's losing. But Spielberg makes a good point about its role as plot development. "You didn't know who the characters were in the first battle—except for Tom Hanks, everybody was anonymous to the audience." Two hours later, that was no longer the case. The audience had invested its time with these soldiers, "the battle was personal and emotional on the part of the audience." It had no choice but to care greatly for the fate of these men whom it had come to care greatly about, perhaps even love—especially, of course, Captain Miller.

He has succeeded in his mission—Private Ryan (Matt Damon) has been found (and is, of course, reluctant to leave

"I think every country should tell stories about their own history. The British have certainly made some of the great stories about World War II. I think that we are responsible for telling as much of what we know and who we are as possible. And we expect that of everyone else who has a story to tell."

his comrades)—but Miller is mortally wounded and as he lies dying near Ryan he mutters his unimprovable last words: "Earn this." Meaning that several men have risked (and lost) their lives to find him and that he owes them a life. And not just any life. Ryan owes them a good life. The movie does not inform us whether he achieves that goal. But we cannot help but think he does. It does not have to be a grand life, full of honors and the good opinion of mankind. It just has to be what Captain Miller's life would have been had he been spared.

Spielberg did not have particularly high hopes for the movie when he finished it; it was just too violent, he judged, for mass popularity. He thought he might get a good first weekend out of it, based on Hanks's appeal. But the box office didn't much matter to him. Along with his cameraman, Janusz Kaminski, and his editor, Michael Kahn, and many of the actors, he "felt like we were making a contribution. I thought the film was going to inform audiences about what soldiers really go through in the hellfire of combat. And that for me was the point: to make this movie as rough and tough as I possibly could, to put those audiences in those combat boots at every single moment along the way of telling the story."

As his rough cut came together, Spielberg could see that he had accomplished that. "It was the most brutal experience I'd had putting violent images on the screen—bodies just torn apart and broken, kind of, you know, losing their souls."

Yet he was haunted by a really horrid thought. "At one point in the movie I turned to Tom Hanks and I said: 'I feel so guilty that I'm having so much fun working on this picture.'" There is one short sequence that is, I think, emblematic of his pleasure. Some German soldiers have been captured and are being led to the rear. A Jewish member of Miller's detachment darts among them waving his dog-tags in their faces, which, of course, carry information about his religious affiliation. He triumphantly cries, "*Juden! Juden!*" at the puzzled captives. It is, in its way, a comical scene. And perhaps an improbable one. Yet it is a powerful one as well.

Perhaps there is another, wider aspect to the enjoyment Spielberg derived from making this film. At some level directors of big action pictures know that what will eventually look horrendous on screen is just trickery and they sometimes take an almost childish delight in pulling the wool over our eyes. Spielberg admits to thinking about the war pictures he made as a suburban kid and reveling now in his mastery of stunts that were so far beyond his innocent eyes back then. Maybe, he concedes, that was part of it, but it doesn't quite explain his sheer exhilaration.

A scene from *Lawrence of Arabia* (a picture he greatly admires) offers him the best explanation he can think of. T.E. Lawrence is standing in a room, making his report to General Allenby about one of his adventures. "There's something else," he says. "Yes?" says Allenby. We notice that Lawrence is shaking. "I shot a man," says Lawrence. It is nothing to the veteran soldier. "You had to do it. It was your duty." "Yes, but there was something more." "What?" "I enjoyed it."

But Spielberg's enjoyment coexisted with something at stake, a message he wanted to send out. *Saving Private Ryan* works so well, ultimately so poignantly, because Miller's little unit is composed of such decent American kids. If there is a fiction in the film it is that there is not one bad apple in the bunch. But that is a fiction we can live with, a fiction that is necessary to us, really, if we are to retain any faith at all in the military necessity, particularly in an age of bad and unnecessary wars. There will come a time, one supposes, when we will have need again for the virtues on display here.

Which are, in Spielberg's view, very simple, almost clichéd ones. For example, "when you talk to veterans they say, 'I can look back and say, sure, I fought the war, you know, to save Western Democracy. But while I was in the thick of it, I fought the war to save my friend, who was in the foxhole right next to me.'" There is no more familiar thought than that when we discuss war nowadays. It can be freshened, made meaningful, only by absolute conviction (and by never expressing it in so many words) of the kind Spielberg brought to this movie.

It's the same way with another of his observations: In modern war—that is to say, televised war—"We don't get personal with those killed or wounded. We don't get to know them. And I wanted to make sure in *Private Ryan* that we got to know the soldiers that we were leaving behind, that were making the supreme sacrifice—that we understood what each individual was leaving behind, that space in everybody's heart that would never be filled again."

In the hands of another director, that could be another less than sophisticated thought. One cannot emphasize it enough: For all his articulateness, for all his technical skills, Steven Spielberg is, at his core, a simple man. That—what shall we call it, morality?—is what he shares with the members of his audience, which, as in the case of *Saving Private Ryan*, helps them overcome their "Oh, it's just another war movie" doubts.

When the movie was released there was a "controversy" about two sequences Spielberg placed at the beginning and the end of the movie. In them, an aging World War II veteran

"From a historical perspective, the Second World War seems really cut and dried, or black and white. But inside a war, and inside combat, it's technically chaotic and personally very chaotic and personally very contradictory. When we look back from the standpoint of history, we can say, 'Oh yeah, World War II clearly set the good and the bad apart from one another.' But inside combat, the issue is never that clear. To the soldiers fighting the war, it can be very confusing."

The modern-day scenes filmed in the Normandy American Cemetery that begin and end the movie struck some reviewers as overly sentimental, but Spielberg strongly disagreed.

is seen searching for a grave in the Normandy American Cemetery. If we think about him at all, as the main action of the movie begins, we guess that he is Private Ryan—rendered unrecognizable by age makeup—and that the grave he is seeking is Captain Miller's.

These sequences were too much for the savagely unsentimental movie critics (who, of course, buy into the worst Hollywood glop most of the time), and they acted as if this was a betrayal of the movie's sternest principles—akin to the little girl in the red coat in *Schindler's List*. Spielberg is dismissive of them.

"If I had to do it all over again, I'd do it the very same way. Because I did that for the veterans. And as a matter of fact it's the veterans who love the bookends, because they put the film in a contemporary context—honoring my dad, honoring all the dads who were part of the greatest generation, by having an old man going to the American Cemetery in Normandy and visiting is amazing, you know. For me I don't think *Private Ryan* could have lived without those bookends."

And, frankly, it's the same for me, too. I have been to that cemetery twice. It never fails to move me, albeit in inexplicable ways. We make room in our movies, in all our fictions, for far more egregious moments of sentiment—

if it even is sentimental, come to think of it. In any case the public bought into it and, for the most part, accepted it quite equally. If they paid much attention to it at all—so rich was the picture in other virtues.

The film, far from Spielberg's expectations, was richly rewarded at the box office, and with all the appropriate nods from the awards-givers. No one, for a long time, had constructed a war movie so spectacularly true to the demands of the genre and yet so honorably true to the demand that it not be a mere shoot-'em-up, that it attempt to say something worthwhile, not about grand aims but about men who are forced into war and must find some value in it or succumb to cynicism or worse. If it is not Spielberg's finest hour, it is surely among them. Because it confronts some of the hoariest clichés of moviedom and by the passion, the ferocity, of Spielberg's attack on them compels our belief—at least for the picture's running time—in the capability, in the capacity, of rather ordinary people to achieve grace under extraordinary pressure. It comes to this, says Spielberg of the fast-vanishing generation this movie celebrates: "You have to understand that these people carry those images with them the rest of their lives. We can just, you know, go buy the movie or rent it, but they've got to live with their memories forever."

A.I.

ARTIFICIAL INTELLIGENCE

(2001)

"I think Stanley Kubrick recognized that the only time our sensibilities were on a parallel track was *A.I.* And Stanley was the one who called me. He was the one who, for the first time ever, said, 'I want you to read a treatment that I've written.'"

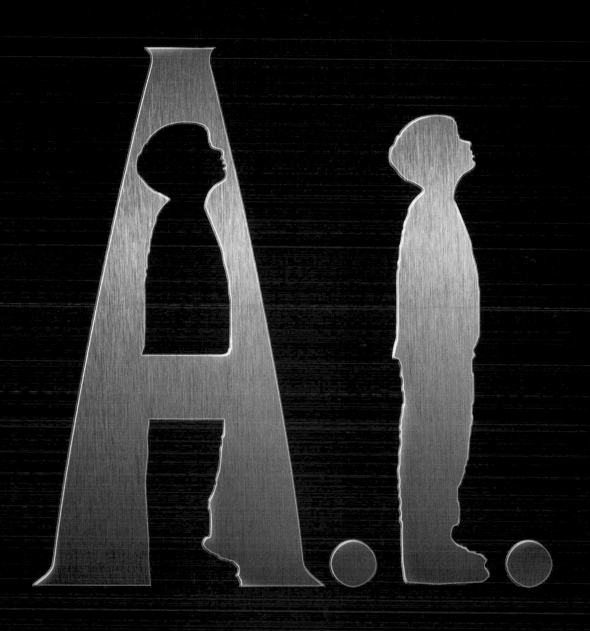

Their collaboration was not without its comical side. Kubrick was an intense man, though nowhere near as crazy as portrayed in the media, which he generally shunned. He was not quite the recluse the journalists thought he was, but he was extraordinarily intelligent, a super-rationalist with only the vaguest relationship to the niceties of time as most people experience it. For example, Spielberg installed a dedicated fax machine for Kubrick's messages in his bedroom, only to find himself awakened at all hours of the night by its chatterings. (His wife soon banished it to another room.) There were occasions when Spielberg found himself engaged in eight-hour phone conversations with Kubrick, noshing lunch and dinner as they proceeded.

He didn't mind at all. Kubrick (whom I knew and liked enormously) was a spellbinder, an irresistible force when he was in full cry, which was much of the time. The story they evolved over the years was, as Kubrick observed, more in Spielberg's territory than his own. The year is 2142, when many coastal cities (New York, Venice, etc.) have been inundated by water. The survivors of this ecological

The making of *A.I.* is a story almost as dramatic as the film itself. A short story by Brian Aldiss, "Supertoys Last All Summer Long," was optioned by Stanley Kubrick sometime in the 1980s and never abandoned by him. Sometime in the 1990s he informally enlisted Spielberg in developing the project, repeatedly insisting that it was better suited to Spielberg's sensibility than his own. That said, however, Kubrick did write a 95-page treatment of the film and commissioned something like 2,000 story boards for it. Spielberg insists that the basic structure of the film was Kubrick's, though he filled in many blanks when, after Kubrick's sudden death in 1999, he wrote the screenplay.

Previous page: The ingenious typography on the poster conveys the movie's replicant theme.

Shooting footage through the eyehole of a mask cast from Haley Joel Osment's face.

disaster, however, are warm and dry inland, where, among other things, they have created a race of robots, outwardly indistinguishable from human beings. These "mechas" are meant to be a serving class. Eventually, Prof. Hobby (William Hurt, whose actorly pomposity for once serves his role admirably) creates the first child replicant, David (Haley Joel Osment). It is determined that David will be adopted by Henry and Monica Swinton, the parents of a child who is being held in a cryostatic coma until a cure for the disease that is afflicting him can be found.

David is, by Spielberg's own admission, the most lost of all his lost boys, in that he is not even a real boy, but a simulacrum of a human being. He is also capable of genuine emotions, which are centered on his love for his surrogate mother, whom Spielberg does not believe really loves the boy. He is a kind of toy for her, a placebo for the child who is in a coma. He, however, is suddenly cured and awakens. And he turns out to be a mean and manipulative child, whose machinations finally drive his mother to abandon David in a dark wood, accompanied only by a walking-talking (and wise) teddy bear, who functions as a kind of Jiminy Cricket in a story that bears more than a passing resemblance to *Pinocchio*. In one of Spielberg's most masterly sequences, David encounters a truly terrifying "Flesh Fair" where humans torture replicants to death. He also comes across

According to Spielberg, Haley Joel Osment gave "one of the greatest performances I've ever had in one of my films." Here in conversation with the director (bottom); and in a tight corner with Jude Law (top), whose performance as Gigolo Joe "perfected dance and movement."

"*A.I.* is about the end of the entire human race that is superseded by the Frankensteins that man has put on the planet in the greedy effort to make a boy who could love you. But the boy himself is not human, he's next to human. A substitute love child, you know, is almost a crime, and the human race pays for that crime. And so I think it's a very tragic story, and I think I was as true to Stanley Kubrick's vision as I possibly could be."

a replicant named Gigolo Joe (Jude Law), who is all that his name implies—a dancing, posturing (and brilliantly portrayed) figure in this drama. They eventually attain a water-logged New York, where David hopes to meet the Blue Fairy, whom he thinks can grant his wish for a mother's love.

He does find her, but by that time he and Teddy are trapped beneath the sea, where for 2,000 years they sleep until they are rescued by some replicants who restore him to life and grant him his wish—a loving encounter with his (digitally recreated) surrogate mother. They have, at last, a perfectly loving day together (no more, no less).

Despite this apparently complex plot, the film actually moves along in a very brisk and coherent way and its moral is quite simple: Love is the most powerful force in the world. It cannot be trifled with. And if its results are, as in this instance, disappointingly modest, they are yet sufficient to satisfy the need of a yearning child (or whatever David is).

Yet that begs some interesting, and modestly controversial, questions, which arose upon the film's release. These most significantly involve the nature of the collaboration between Spielberg and Kubrick, and whose vision was more potent in shaping the final film.

The ending is where the most intense interest centers. "People assume that Stanley ended *A.I.* with David and Teddy underwater, trapped by the Ferris wheel," Spielberg says, "and that they're going to be down there until their batteries run out and the end credits roll.

"That's where they assume Stanley ended it and I, of course, get criticized for carrying the film 2,000 years into the future, where the robots we've created have replaced us and super-mechas rule the world. They assume that's how I wrecked Stanley's movie, when, in fact, Stanley's treatment went right into the 2,000-year future, right into every single beat that I put into my version of Stanley's story. I wrote the screenplay because Stanley wasn't alive to make the movie. Those were Stanley's ideas."

Which come to their most violent and intense focus at the Flesh Fair. Spielberg thought he could well have made an entire movie centered on that Holocaust-like event with the humans exterminating the mechas "because they were so afraid of losing their identities, losing their jobs, to a race of serving men and women—all these poor, helpless mechas." He insists that Kubrick's story boards made this sequence look like a twenty-second-century Holocaust.

During their journey to New York, David and Teddy (bottom) encounter all kinds of obstacles, including the horrific "Flesh Fair." When finally they reach their destination, they discover a city consumed by the sea (top).

More important, it posed the movie's most basic question in the starkest, most vividly violent terms. "It's questioning the audience about the difference between sentient behavior and the behavior of a doll. Where is your moral judgment going to fall? How are you going to judge creatures that look and act just like us?

"You know," Spielberg adds, "I think a lot of people took offense to the basic precepts of artificial intelligence—can you love something that was made by the person next door? Can you love your doll, can you love your Barbies, and, yes, you can, when you are a child. But can a mother love a Barbie doll who looks and acts just like a real kid?"

This is actually a profound question, the kind of question, indeed, that Kubrick more than Spielberg was wont to ask. The latter's best movies, I think, pose answerable questions. Their morality asks relatively straightforward questions of the kind that people of normal sensibilities agree upon. *A.I.* is not a movie of that type. It is an open-ended film. We are free to feel that if a creature like David quacks like a duck he is a duck for all intents and purposes. Conversely, we are free to believe that he is composed of a hundred miles of wires and circuitry, which makes no allowance for a soul. Therefore, we are free to abuse him and his kind in any way that we choose. We can abandon them. We can trash them. With impunity.

But, of course, no one has identified the place of the soul in the human anatomy. We take it on faith. Or we do not. Which raises the central, existential conundrum of our lives—to which we have no answer. The more humanistically inclined Spielberg was obviously prepared to accept the possibility that David had achieved full-scale humanity. He seems to argue that Kubrick was in agreement with him. I'm not so sure of that. His was an altogether darker sensibility, which is why, I think, he kept urging Spielberg to direct the film. It's possible that perhaps he just couldn't find it in his heart to embrace the film's ambiguously happy ending—though Spielberg insists that the concept of achieving one perfect day for the surrogate mother and her adopted child was, from the start, part of Kubrick's plan for the film.

Perhaps, in the end, it doesn't matter. The film is, as I have previously suggested, a relatively straightforward story of a boy (you can't help but think of him in human terms) seeking love that is withheld for what amounts to eternity and receiving only the paltriest of rewards in the end. But the plotting is, however, brilliant in its complexity and its capacity to surprise, with its sudden turns toward terror and heartbreak and dark humor. And the acting, particularly by Jude Law and Haley Joel Osment, is astonishing. Of the former, Spielberg says, "He perfected

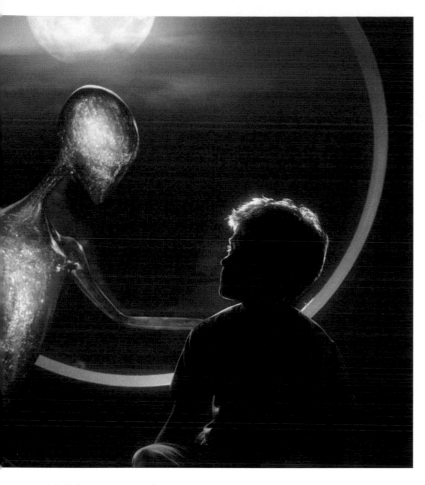

dance and movement ... the way he turned his head and moved his hands. There wasn't a single wasted movement in that performance." Yet this is not merely a technical accomplishment. He is, at once, a sinister gigolo, a soft-shoe artist, and a kind of dark vaudevillian, with, sometimes, a beating heart for his boy companion.

As for Haley Joel Osment, he gives what Spielberg considers to be "one of the greatest performances I've ever had in one of my films." And a hard-nosed one; he never asks for sympathy or shows fear or compromises his quest, he just keeps forging gamely ahead. It is said that Osment was the one who proposed that his character never blink—literally, never. It's the only indication that he's not entirely human.

Kubrick had thought David—perhaps all the mechas—should be rendered digitally. And, in retrospect, Spielberg, for all his admiration of Osment's work, agrees. It would have been more disconcerting, something for the audience to conjure with uncomfortably. But the state of the art—and this was just a trifle over a decade ago—was not at that stage yet. Dinosaurs, yes; humanoids, no.

In the end I don't think it mattered much. It's the sort of what-might-have-been that filmmakers brood about occasionally, but audiences, content with what they have (when the movie is good), don't care greatly about. My own judgment is that *A.I.* is perhaps Spielberg's most complex and difficult film   the one that raises the questions that are the hardest to answer. It is also, despite its many softening felicities (Spielberg can never completely still his impulse to charm, though he can, as he does here, keep it in check), a harsh and largely uncompromising film. That "happy" ending is not so very happy, come to think of it. And along the way to it the human race is presented in an ugly light. The irony is that it is the mechas who are portrayed as the kindly humanists, which is a Kubrickian, not a Spielbergian, trope. To come right down to it, the movie needs whatever warmth Spielberg can bring to it, else it would be close to unbearable.

Which it is not. It was greeted on the whole approvingly by the critics—the line was that it was a chilly film, but one that took up serious and ambiguous issues in a mature fashion. No one mistook it for an exercise in warmth—or a desperate effort to find more of that quality than was inherent in the story. It did reasonably well at the worldwide box office, as it deserved to do. It is not a movie that, frankly, I looked forward to re-encountering for the purposes of this book. But I'm glad I did. It turns out that Spielberg is more than capable of embracing that which is forever unanswerable. Stanley Kubrick, had he lived to see the work, would have approved of it.

MINORITY REPORT

(2002)

"It's a popcorn movie—
but a gourmet popcorn movie."

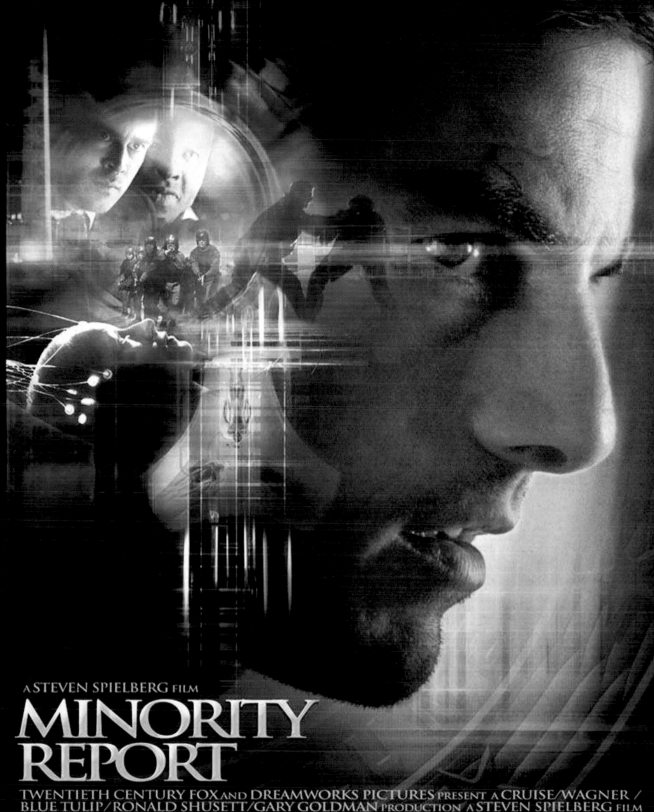

"I always wanted to do a George Orwell style of story because I loved *1984*, which I read when I was young," says Spielberg. He also wanted to do something in the vein of a Humphrey Bogart-Lauren Bacall film noir mystery-detective story, a genre he had not previously explored. He thought *Minority Report*, a script he had worked on first with Jon Cohen, then with Scott Frank for quite a long time, offered possibilities of both kinds. It does have an arresting premise. The year is 2054 and Washington, D.C. is basically free of, as it were, capital crimes.

Above: Spielberg would reprise his partnership with Tom Cruise three years later for *War of the Worlds*.

Left: Spielberg's first post-9/11 movie was a reflection on the boundary between government authority and civil liberty.

Previous page: The US poster for Spielberg's take on an Orwellian film noir.

That's because three psychic "pre-cogs," floating in a tank of fluid, are able to pre-visualize crimes, dispatching teams of policemen to the potential crime scene, to prevent any mayhem before it happens. A wonderfully athletic Tom Cruise is John Anderton, the finest of the finest among the crime fighters. Samantha Morton is Agatha, the most acute of the pre-cogs.

Cruise, however, is a haunted man. His beloved son has been abducted at a swimming pool and he has no idea of the boy's fate, which leads him to divorce and depression. Now, with this program on the verge of going national, Agatha determines that he is just 36 hours away from committing murder himself, his presumptive victim being a man he does not know. He must, among other things, try to recover a "minority report," which predicts an outcome alternative to the one Agatha has envisioned.

Minority Report is, at its most basic level, a thrillingly orchestrated succession of chases and action set pieces. Spielberg has never been better than he is with these sequences, and the film is photographed by Janusz Kaminski in effectively eerie bluish tones. It also has a more or less conventional plot, in which a kindly-looking Max von Sydow is trying to subvert the program and kills eager-beaver Colin Farrell when he uncovers his plan.

There is a particularly wonderful sequence where Anderton and Agatha must negotiate a shopping mall without being discovered. It depends on perfect timing—a balloon, for instance, hiding them from watching eyes as they make their passage. And amusing asides. At one point, Agatha warns a passing pedestrian not to go home that night. "He knows," she tells the startled woman.

But the movie has higher intentions: It wants to ask, Spielberg says, "How many of our civil liberties are we willing to give up because the government tells us we have to in order to protect us from terrorism in the shadow, the aftermath, of 9/11?" The movie, at its highest level, is asking questions about free will. "Does the government have the legal right literally to put you out of commission for the rest of your life because of a murder you haven't committed, but that the government is certain you will?" Spielberg asks. "Look, knowledge of what's going to happen even five minutes from now will give you ultimate power. There is no greater power than foretelling the future. Left to her own devices, Agatha, as a pre-cog, could rule the world."

She does not, of course. Pre-cogs are, thank God, an amusing and thought-provoking fiction. But the United States government—or the government of any modern nation state—has vast resources for looking into our secrets.

On set with Tom Cruise: Spielberg had been looking for the right opportunity to work with Cruise since they first met in the early 1980s. He almost directed him in *Rain Man*, but left to work on *Indiana Jones and the Last Crusade* instead.

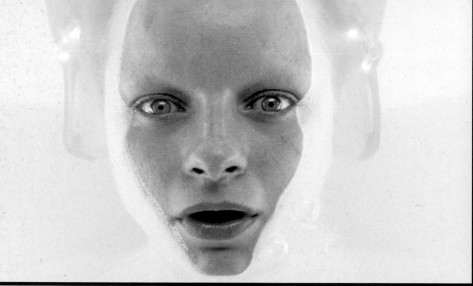

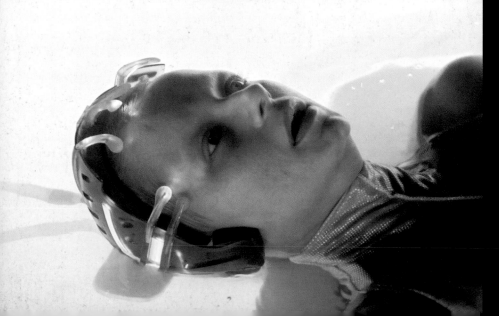

"Science fiction loves to warn. Remember, science fiction has always been a kind of first-level alert to think about things to come. It's easier for an audience to heed warnings from sci-fi without feeling that we're preaching to them."

It is clumsy, bureaucratic, and duplicative; it must, in its bumbling way, miss a lot of opportunities for mischief. But the machinery is there, and it is probably refining its efforts right now.

That does not mean that *Minority Report* is an altogether successful movie. It functions best at the thriller level. As long as Cruise is chasing madly around—at one point he swaps his eyes for another set (they are used for recognition purposes by machines that guard the portals of secret sites)—it is an engaging, exciting movie. But it is also a very complicated one. It has a lot of business in hand and some of it is conducted rather hastily. We lack, at times, the fuller explanations that would satisfy our deepest curiosity. That happens a lot in movies nowadays. This one, for example, is well over two hours in length and you end up somewhat exhausted, but not fully satisfied, by it (the machinations of von Sydow's character seem to me particularly at fault in this respect). Also, along the way, I think it largely fails as film noir. It has the look of such a film, but generally fails to provide the witty badinage of, say, Bogart and Bacall in full bantering cry—this is because the love interest, between Cruise and his divorced wife, is of a regretful and somewhat under-developed nature.

It may be that it just has too much on its plate, too much, at any rate, to satisfy us at every level it aspires to. But, of course, it is better to try for too much than for too little, which is much more common in movies these days. And audiences didn't seem to care. They essentially got off on the film's thrill-ride aspects. At that, most basic, level, it seemed to work for them. And in worldwide release it grossed extremely well.

It is not a great film, but it is not nothing either. It is, as they say, "a good ride" and an entertainment that poses, without conclusively answering, some interesting questions about the intrusions of government on the lives of our citizens.

Agatha: "I'm sorry John, but you're gonna have to run again." Tom Cruise (John Anderton) and Samantha Morton (Agatha) rehearse their next move.

Previous page: The pre-cogs float in a womb-like pool, where their thoughts are harvested for crime-prevention purposes.

CATCH ME IF YOU CAN

(2002)

"Leo had such a wily intelligence in his eyes, he had such a great presentational style. Frank got away with everything he got away with based on 80 percent presentation, only 20 percent imagination. It's all about presentation."

"*Catch Me If You Can* was, for me, a breath of fresh air," says Spielberg. It was the pretty much true story of one Frank Abagnale, Jr., a teenaged con artist who, in the course of a short but very lively career, posed as an airline pilot, a doctor, and a lawyer the better to kite something like four million dollars in bad checks. As played by Leonardo DiCaprio, he's a smooth, but not necessarily humorous, operator, whose pleasure in his deceptions is only rarely marked by smugness or good cheer, which is very much to this movie's advantage. This guy's business is too serious for light-mindedness, which is also to his advantage, especially since his chief pursuer is his opposite, Tom Hanks's wonderfully geeky and obsessive FBI agent, Carl Hanratty.

Previous page and right: Living the high life. As Frank Abagnale, Jr., Leonardo DiCaprio is a master of deception and disguise.

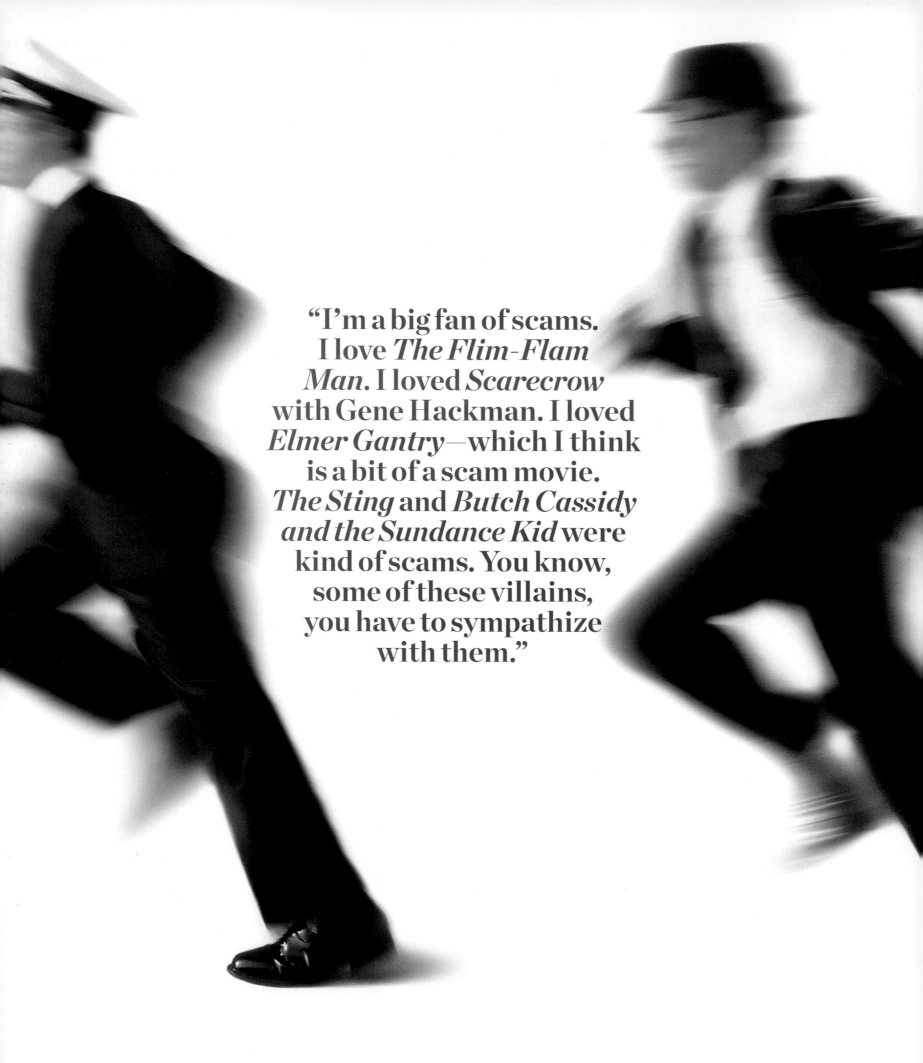

"I'm a big fan of scams. I love *The Flim-Flam Man*. I loved *Scarecrow* with Gene Hackman. I loved *Elmer Gantry*—which I think is a bit of a scam movie. *The Sting* and *Butch Cassidy and the Sundance Kid* were kind of scams. You know, some of these villains, you have to sympathize with them."

Hanks wears decidedly wonky eyeglasses and silly little hats and is often to be found alone in his office on Christmas Eve, distractedly eating Chinese food and focusing on the elusive Abagnale. He has a busted marriage, a squawking Boston accent, and a developing fondness for his prey.

The movie is not particularly interested in developing motives for Abagnale's activities. He is, in fact, another one of Spielberg's lost boys, wandering through the universe looking for some kind of identity he can latch on to. Or, to be more precise, a reliable father figure. What he has, instead, is a dad who is himself a small-time artist of deals that perpetually go wrong. Brilliantly played by Christopher Walken, with his patented blend of earnestness and restrained loopiness, he is introduced as a man winning a Rotary Club good-citizenship award, although he is already engaged in a movie-long struggle with the IRS over non-payment of taxes. If the movie has a love story, it is between the Abagnales, senior and junior, with the older man sort of pleased that his son has far surpassed him in the family calling, but also refusing to profit from the kid's success.

At this late date, it is doubtless safe to reveal that Hanratty finally runs Abagnale, Jr., to ground in the little French village where his father met his sexy, essentially unreliable mother at the end of World War II. He sees to it that Abagnale is tried and imprisoned—but then permits him to go straight, working for the FBI to catch others of his ilk and (a closing title informs us) making a small fortune by inventing various instruments that prevent, or at least harass, others who would perpetuate frauds of the kind he once specialized in. Happy (and truthful) endings all around.

"When I met the real Frank Abagnale," says Spielberg, "and saw the force of his personality, the second I met him I said, 'He could pull the wool over anyone's eyes.'" The film was generally well reviewed, though some critics wanted it to be a merrier chase than it actually was—one of those genial con-man movies where nothing is at stake but a lot of mislaid money, no harm done. There are traces of that in the story, of course, but, for the most part, the audience is encouraged to irony, and a certain amount of fairly mild suspense, not so much to outright hilarity.

Opposite: With its glamorous costumes, performers, and locations, *Catch Me If You Can* is seen by many as nothing more than a light caper movie, but strong on irony.

"He's an amazing master of deception and disguise," Spielberg says, "but he reminded me a little bit of Oskar Schindler in a strange way." What way? "Just his command of being able to deceive people into believing his agenda was their agenda, when, in fact, he had a totally different agenda. Oskar Schindler toyed with the Nazi party, deceived them into believing he was one of them. When, in fact, he was making off with a lot of their money and was about to do one of the greatest righteous things any human being could possibly do—being the great deceiver in order to give the Jews a safe haven."

I hadn't thought of that.

"I just thought of it sitting here. That's what happens sometimes in an interview. I see things I never saw before. I think I saw that for the first time sitting here."

A slightly alarming prospect is gently raised at this point: that all movies, even the most sober and aspiring of them, have about them an element of the con. Their most basic aim, after all, is to put bottoms in the chairs in the theaters. This is scarcely a crime or even a misdemeanor. It is a game everyone plays. Without malice. So, as in the case of *Catch Me If You Can*, if the customers are encouraged to see the movie as a lighter, more genial movie than it is, what harm is done? Good memories are served. Value is received. Respectable profits are turned. And Spielberg has another movie that he has reason to be proud of. With his very next project he would pull off the same trick, perhaps even more delightfully.

Above: Spielberg and DiCaprio approve the dailies.

Right: Leonardo DiCaprio checks for another escape route while in conversation with the director and Tom Hanks.

TOM HANKS
Catherine Zeta-Jones

A STEVEN SPIELBERG Film

The Terminal

Life is waiting.

DREAMWORKS PICTURES presents A PARKES/MacDONALD Production A STEVEN SPIELBERG Film
TOM HANKS CATHERINE ZETA-JONES "THE TERMINAL" STANLEY TUCCI CHI McBRIDE DIEGO LUNA
Casting by DEBRA ZANE, C.S.A. Produced by SERGIO MIMICA GEZZAN Music by JOHN WILLIAMS Costume Designer MARY ZOPHRES Editor MICHAEL KAHN, A.C.E.
Production Designer ALEX McDOWELL Director of Photography JANUSZ KAMINSKI, ASC Executive Producers PATRICIA WHITCHER JASON HOFFS ANDREW NICCOL
Produced by WALTER F. PARKES LAURIE MacDONALD STEVEN SPIELBERG Story by ANDREW NICCOL and SACHA GERVASI Screenplay by SACHA GERVASI and JEFF NATHANSON
Directed by STEVEN SPIELBERG

THE TERMINAL

(2004)

"I wanted to do a movie
that could make us laugh
and cry and feel good
about the world."

Previous page: As Viktor Navorski, a slightly bulky refugee trapped in an airport terminal, Tom Hanks gives what Spielberg considers to be his finest movie performance.

Spielberg thought the script by Jeff Nathanson and Sacha Gervasi was charming and original, "a fish out of water story" about one Viktor Navorski, resident of the fictional country of Krakozhia, who becomes stateless—through a political coup—while flying into the United States and is forced to become a resident of the eponymous airport building, unable to go about his innocent business in this country and unable to return to his homeland either. He especially wanted to do the film if Tom Hanks would play Viktor. It would be, come to think of it, a triumph of off-casting, because, as Spielberg says, "Tom is quintessentially America's favorite son—he has basically created himself as the most iconically American actor that we have working in movies today."

Now he would be asked to play a slightly bulked-up, heavily accented character who is entirely innocent of American ways—and more. He is trapped in an environment most of us pass through on autopilot, without even stopping to think if there is anything like a life going on there. Putting it briefly, he would be playing the exact opposite of what he had always represented on the screen.

When the picture came out, reviewers noticed this, obviously—how could they not?—but I don't think they made as much of Hanks's turnabout as they might have. Spielberg did. "I frankly and selfishly think it's the best performance Tom has ever given in a movie, including *Forrest Gump* and the character he played in *Philadelphia*. For which he won Oscars. That's my humble opinion, being the director with no objectivity here."

Viktor keeps applying to Stanley Tucci's Homeland Security official for relief of his situation, and the latter's grumpiness does give way to a certain sympathy, but no real helpfulness. Essentially, Viktor is a no man in a no man's land—a universal refugee. But he is also a clever and ingratiating fellow, learning to survive in a seemingly unyielding and plasticized world.

Take eating, for example. Saltine crackers are available, and condiments. He makes a kind of happy face out of mustard, ketchup, and mayonnaise, which becomes his first, very humble dinner. Then there's the matter of the luggage carts. They're worth a quarter when they are returned. When he returns enough of them he can afford to buy a burger at Burger King. And so on up the ladder, until he has a crew working for him, doing repairs on the building. And he conducts a shy little romance with Catherine Zeta-Jones as an airline hostess who passes frequently through the building exuding a mysteriously unhappy air.

An Iranian emigrant named Mehran Karimi Nasseri lived for nearly 18 years in Charles de Gaulle Airport, Paris, on a basis similar to Viktor's, and, indeed, DreamWorks paid $250,000 for rights to his story, though it seems nothing more than his general situation was drawn upon for the screenplay. Frank Capra and "his honest sentiment" was more on Spielberg's mind. And Jacques Tati, too—who "was all about resourcefulness and using what was around him to make us laugh."

What was around Hanks and the other actors did not come cheap. There was no way the filmmakers could borrow

"I believe all of us have felt a little bit like Viktor at some time in our lives— this displaced person in search of a life."

Viktor's ordeal begins to take its toll, but he displays an incredible resilience and resourcefulness as the movie develops.

an existing terminal and shoot in its off hours. So they built one in a disused airplane hangar in Palmdale, California— 60 feet tall, 100,000 square feet in area, employing 200 workers for 20 weeks of construction—and, one must say, it is a marvel of realism. And all, essentially, to showcase Hanks's performance. Which, as Spielberg says, was not "a part of an ensemble cast, but a tour de force opportunity."

People who write about movies noticed that after a string of dark, or at least very serious, films (*Amistad, Saving Private Ryan, A.I., Minority Report*) Spielberg had, with *Catch Me If You Can* and *The Terminal*, "embraced my return to my youthful exuberance—lighter, frothier fare. And I was relieved to get away from the dark side of my own impulses and to do those films literally back to back." But, he wryly notes, when he made *War of the Worlds* and *Munich* next "people totally forgot that I ever made the two light movies in the middle of this dark act."

But, he says, this balancing of light and dark isn't a conscious thing with him. "I don't plan. I don't say, 'OK, now I just have to make light, popcorn movies to give them relief from whatever my subconscious demons are that have pushed me into darker, more historical subjects.' I don't think that way. I do whatever comes along, when its time has come."

This is an important, and often overlooked, point. Steven Spielberg is not a total filmmaker. As we've seen, there are some kinds of films that he is not comfortable making, whether they be raucous comedies like *1941*, or soft romances like *Always*, or totally odd ventures like *Hook*. But it must be said that alone among contemporary filmmakers he has three distinct sides to his career.

Most directors rather quickly find their sweet spots. They make comedies, for instance. Or action pictures. Or romances. They may occasionally venture from their chosen genres, but these films are indulgences, something the studios allow them to make against the promise of a return to their home territory. But Spielberg is a proven expert in fairly straightforward action pictures (*Jaws, Jurassic Park*), in humanistic dramas like *E.T.*, and, of course, in serious films on topics that are deeply meaningful to him (*Schindler's List, The Color Purple*, et al.).

He is, in short, hard to pigeon-hole, elusive. And I think that puzzles critics and maybe audiences as well. They're not complaining, of course. They have rewarded him more richly than perhaps any other director in the history of the medium. There is a built-in "want to see" with every project he announces, and a tolerant understanding that it will

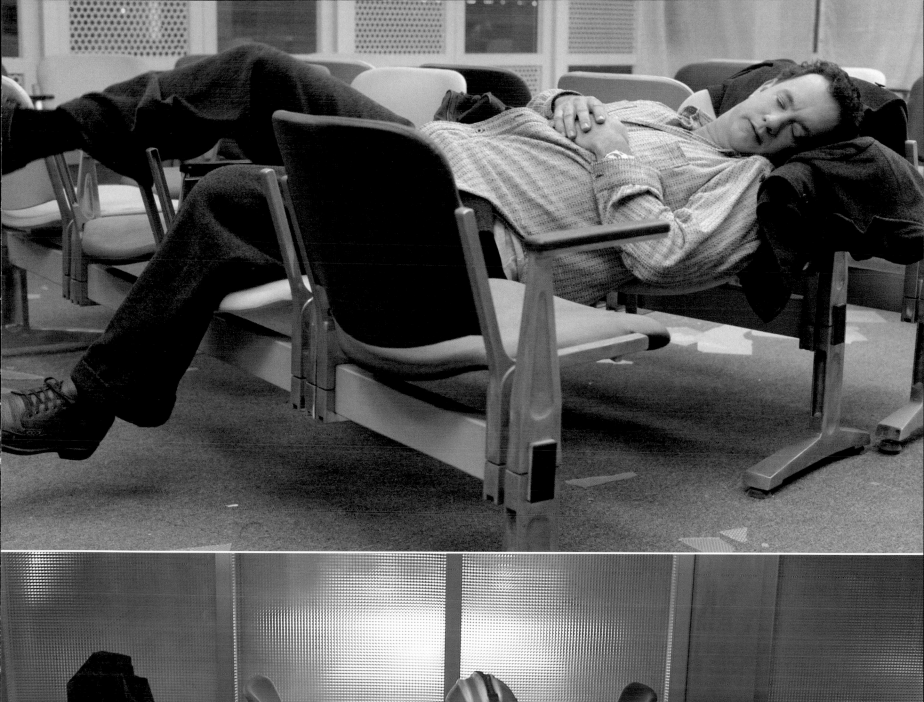

at least be worthy of their attention. But, well, "neatness counts." Or, at least, predictability. I think the sheer range of his interests prevents people from fully acknowledging his place in the film world. He is, if you will, a force of nature—someone whose unpredictability is the only predictable thing about him. It would be impossible—no, ludicrous—to feel sorry for him. But I do think his range and fecundity at some, admittedly minor, level prevents serious film commentators from taking him entirely seriously. If you go through the reviews of his work, there is a "yes, but" quality to some of them, or, conversely, a sort of shrugging attitude, that does not attend the work of more narrowly focused auteurs. The fact that he is always aiming at the widest possible audience—that he does not make "art"

The polished floors of the remarkably realistic, but completely artificial, terminal building were great for scootering around on, but not so hot for stilettos.

"It's a fantasy. It's a Frank Capra movie. I always thought that when we made *The Terminal*, we were also taking our hats off to Capra."

movies, that he always intends his movies to make money—does not help his cause, either. This is probably the fate of all populists. He has, as we have had reasons to explore, his themes, his obsessions, which he returns to time and time again. It's just that he generally hides them better than most—under an air of carefully tended normalcy—in both his professional and private lives.

Be that as it may, I think *The Terminal* is among his most charming movies, with Hanks in particularly delicate form. He's a go-getter of causes, wittily solving problems as simple as getting enough to eat, as complex as making a living in limbo. But there is something wistful about him, too—almost yearning. He is, essentially, lovable—but without ever suing us for our sentimental regard.

A transparently decent man, Viktor soon earns the love and respect of the whole community of terminal workers.

WAR OF THE WORLDS

(2005)

"I never made *War of the Worlds* for a family audience. *War of the Worlds* was a very intense post-9/11 apocalyptic movie about the end of everything."

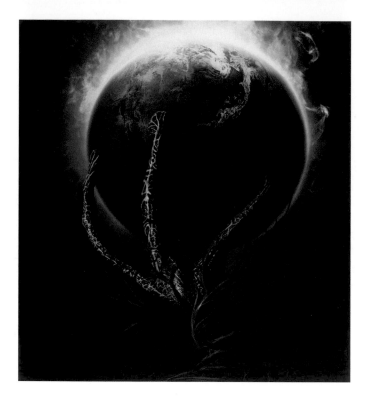

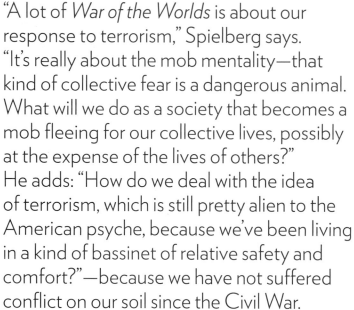

"A lot of *War of the Worlds* is about our response to terrorism," Spielberg says. "It's really about the mob mentality—that kind of collective fear is a dangerous animal. What will we do as a society that becomes a mob fleeing for our collective lives, possibly at the expense of the lives of others?" He adds: "How do we deal with the idea of terrorism, which is still pretty alien to the American psyche, because we've been living in a kind of bassinet of relative safety and comfort?"—because we have not suffered conflict on our soil since the Civil War.

Previous page and opposite: An ordinary man in an extraordinary situation—Tom Cruise signs up for another white-knuckle ride.

Above: The menacing poster image shows the world in the grip of an alien power—a far cry from lovable E.T.

And besides: "The oceans don't seem so vast anymore. The computer and the cell phone have reduced our world to the size of a sound bite, and all this information makes us feel more vulnerable than ever before, and I think *War of the Worlds* preyed on our fears and vulnerabilities."

To deal with these issues required a large-scale reimagination of H.G. Wells' 1898 novel and its many subsequent adaptations in other media. These were told in what might be termed a "top-down" way, from the viewpoint of scientists and officials impotently struggling against the super-intelligent intruders from outer space. What was required now was what might be termed a more populist view of the battle.

To that end, Spielberg and screenwriters David Koepp and Josh Friedman came up with an ordinary fellow called Ray Ferrier (Tom Cruise), a somewhat feckless dockworker who has custody of his children, Rachel (Dakota Fanning) and Robbie (Justin Chatwin), on the weekend the aliens show their hand. They have to develop and demonstrate their survival skills—mostly by running in an all-fired hurry.

The aliens, too, are different from the Wells' version. They buried their really large, really scary killing machines below ground thousands of years earlier, awaiting their emergence in the light, which, for no particular reason, occurs on the day when Ray is looking for something to occupy his kids.

Both of these inventions strike me as advantageous to the movie. The knowledge that the aliens have been planning this invasion for millennia is a clear indication of their intelligence and complete meanness of spirit, a warning that they may be unstoppably malevolent. And the notion that Cruise and his kids are only average-bright lends them a vulnerability that enlists our sympathy for their plight. They are game enough, but they—not to mention the rest of humanity—are, seemingly, disastrously over-matched in this contest.

The movie is rich in terrifying incident, one of those Spielberg movies that is, essentially, one damn thing after another. It is all expertly staged and very well acted—by Cruise in particular, as "a deadbeat father who's not very good with his kids and has to become a pretty great dad pretty quickly in order to save their lives and protect his little world from falling apart. I thought that brought the audience into the film more than if it had been told from the point of view of the Joint Chiefs of Staff or the Vice President. It's to Tom's credit as an actor that he can become, right before your eyes, a very ordinary guy filled with parental flaws."

"Science fiction is not a subconscious thing at all; to me it's a vacation. It's a vacation away from all the rules of narrative logic; it's a vacation away from physics and physical science. It lets you leave all the rules behind and fly."

Although a reimagining of H.G. Wells'
novel, the movie preserves details
from the book, including the red alien
weed that spreads over the landscape
suffocating indigenous flora and fauna.

Spielberg says that in real life Cruise is an "amazing, perfect dad, so for him to take the leap, to play an imperfect dad was a very interesting thing to do." As, indeed, it was. Cruise has always been a better actor than he is generally given credit for and his performance here provides the picture with a human interest that it would not, perhaps, have had with another actor in the role.

And that says nothing about the flaming train. It sometimes happens that a routinely expert thriller is transformed into something truly memorable by a single transformative shot, and that was the case here. One day Spielberg was pre-visualizing his movie at his computer, "and I thought, what if they get to the ferry and there's a train that goes through—the gates come down and the people stop, and there's a runaway train, completely covered in flames. And when it clears the people walk to the ferry." The idea was simply to suggest that "a lot more is happening that we're not showing the audience, that there's a whole other world being destroyed five miles in that direction and that there's a city being demolished and razed ten miles in another direction. There are all sorts of things that are being embraced by other fathers and mothers, because I wanted people to think it was a bigger story than just this family."

The shot is very brief, and it is interesting that the stunned crowd at the crossing does not particularly register shock and awe as the train thunders through. By this time they have absorbed so much improbable horror that when the train passes and the gates rise they just keep shuffling on to … wherever. (Spielberg's handling of scenes like this was very much influenced by newsreel footage of Parisians hitting the roads out of Paris after the German occupation of the city in the early days of World War II.)

The shot does not "save" the picture: It is not in need of saving. It is, though, a signature moment, the first image we remember when we think back on *War of the Worlds* now, this expert and commercially successful movie that is what none of its predecessors was—a celebration of "family values" in highly unlikely circumstances. No one will mistake it for a "major" Spielberg offering. But it is an entertaining reversion—skillful and exciting—to an earlier vein, which he had not revisited for close to a decade. And it was highly successful at the box office.

One of the alien spacecraft catches Dakota Fanning full beam.

MUNICH

(2005)

"This movie is a prayer for peace. I was always thinking about that as I was making the picture."

"That's the key phrase for me—'unintended consequences.'" Spielberg is talking about *Munich*, a film that is, at once, a thriller, and, yes, a meditation on how humanity sometimes wins out in even the most desperate circumstances. The thriller aspect first: At the 1972 Olympic Games in Munich, elements of Black September, a terrorist group operating out of Palestine, took hostage and ultimately murdered 11 members of the Israeli team. This crime could not, of course, go unanswered, so Golda Meir, the Israeli prime minister, established several teams of secret agents charged with making reprisals on the terrorists.

Above: Spielberg directs Lynn Cohen playing Israeli prime minister Golda Meir as she follows the terrorist attack on TV (right). The death toll is plain to see on the cover of the *Jerusalem Post* (left).

This film follows the fate of one such team, headed by Avner (Eric Bana), other members of which include the future James Bond, Daniel Craig, and Ciarán Hinds. They are soon, and successfully, tracking down their quarries in various corners of Europe and the Middle East. At this level, the movie functions as a first-class suspense thriller, charged with hair's-breadth, and occasionally bloody, incident.

But the film has another level, which seems to me unique in the history of espionage dramas. That, for want of a better phrase, is the element of doubt that creeps into Avner's mind as he and his group pursue their mission over a longer period of time than they anticipated. In essence, Avner is eventually "struggling to keep his soul intact," Spielberg says. By which he means this: "You keep going because you believe in the mission, and because you love your country and you're the team leader. But there is something about killing people at close range—people who are leading double lives and look perfectly reasonable and civilized when they are not killing people. There's something about that that is going to test a man's soul. I really feel Avner all through the story struggles to keep his soul intact."

This theme is presented in a particularly poignant scene, where the young daughter of a terrorist returns to the family apartment to retrieve some school work she has left behind. While there, the phone rings. She thinks to pick it up—not knowing that it is rigged with a bomb intended to blow up her father, who awaits her in a car on the street below. She is an innocent, ignorant of his secret terrorist life. She is also, potentially, an "unintended consequence" of the events this film relates.

She escapes. Others do not. Especially Avner. Asked whether this man can ever find peace after the events he has participated in, Spielberg, who came to know Avner when the story was undergoing its lengthy development, responds: "No, never. I don't think so. I think something like this changes you forever. I don't think he'll ever find peace."

Avner's troubled conscience is symbolized in a sequence where he is trying to make love to his wife, who has become estranged from him because of his obsession with his endless mission. This attempt at sexual reconciliation is frustrated because horrific images of the violence he and others have committed keep entering his mind.

Opposite: The director mirrors the reflective pose adopted by Avner (Eric Bana) on the film's poster (page 233).

Above: Avner and his team get to work. From left to right: Daniel Craig, Eric Bana, Ciarán Hinds, Mathieu Kassovitz, and Hanns Zischler.

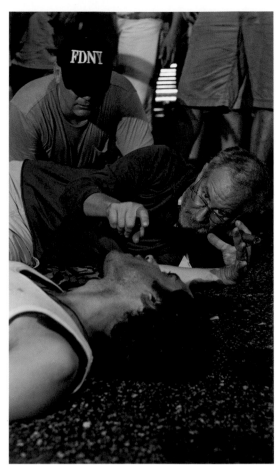

Getting down
to street level:
Munich was
shot on location
in various
European cities,
including Paris
and Budapest.

This, however, was not a movie that Spielberg came to easily. His partner, Kathleen Kennedy, had acquired the rights to a book by George Jonas called *Vengeance*, an account of the known facts of the revenge mission. The book was "controversial" in that many of its precise details will not be known until files are unsealed sometime in the future. Many members of Mossad (the Israeli secret service) were angered by it. On the other hand, Spielberg insists that in broad outline the book is true, though the film went out labeled as "based" on a true story.

In any case, after denying the film several times, Spielberg finally involved himself in the development process. Several writers worked on screenplay drafts, to no good effect. Then, impressed by the HBO miniseries *Angels in America*, which Tony Kushner had adapted from his own award-winning play, Spielberg and Kennedy approached its gifted author and enlisted him in their cause. Kushner not only wrote the final script, but stayed at Spielberg's side throughout the shoot, in several countries.

There was no question between them that Golda Meir had done the right thing in launching the campaign against the terrorists. "I frankly don't think that any Israeli government could have done anything less," Spielberg says. On the other hand, it was vital to Spielberg that Avner, in particular, not be seen as a sort of Charles Bronson figure.

"I certainly didn't want to make my version of *Death Wish*, based on these real, historical events."

This is, of course, where the second, and to Spielberg the most important, theme of *Munich* shines forth. "The movie offers a forum—there are some people in the Jewish community who don't think it was appropriate to have a given position on, or even a scene to explore, the Palestinian character. But Tony and I thought it was very, very important. There's been a quagmire of blood for blood for many decades in that region. And where does it end? How can it end? This movie is a prayer for peace."

This idea is stated most poignantly in a fictional scene entirely of Kushner's invention. In it, Avner and his Palestinian counterpart meet briefly. In effect, the scene says, everyone needs a home and the Palestinians really don't have one. The movie is saying—among other things, of course—that this has to be worked out.

Though, of course, as Spielberg says, "I don't think any movie or any book or any work of art can solve the stalemate in the Middle East today. I think the only thing that's going to solve this is rational minds, a lot of conversation, a lot of sitting down and talking until you're blue in the face."

Which, in some sense is what happened to Spielberg when he was directing *Munich*. He says that "banging around inside my brain while I was making *Munich*"

were such modern-day thrillers as Fred Zinnemann's *The Day of the Jackal*, Costa-Gavras's *Z*, and Gillo Pontecorvo's *The Battle of Algiers*. "It was never meant to go out there and create this sort of political ruckus. It was also meant to be a political thriller."

It functions, as we have observed, very well on that level. But there is something else about it that is, I think, quite unique in movies of this type. For all its geographical range, for all the large issues it raises, it is quite an intimate movie. A lot of the time it consists of small groups of men sitting around in dark rooms talking about this and that. When that observation was conveyed to Spielberg, he became excited: "You're absolutely right. You're absolutely right. That's exactly right. That's exactly right. In a way this is as close as I've ever come to directing a play, and I was well aware of that."

He was aware of something else, too—because Kushner was particularly conscious of it. They thought people, particularly in the Jewish community, were not going to appreciate the message implicit in the film. Yes, of course, at some level the affirmation of the need to take action against the perpetrators of the Munich crimes would strike a chord. But they thought the film would be, to use Kushner's word, "swift-boated," despite the universal recognition that, at the end of the day, however long it takes, the

Palestinians and the Israelis will have to come to some sort of accommodation. Kushner was right to fear that *Munich* would be smeared. Liberal and Conservative Jewish leaders, on the whole, did not like the film; the op-ed pages were rife with their opposition. It was, says Spielberg, middle-of-the-road Jews who responded positively to the movie's reconciliatory spirit—especially since there was never any doubt about the film's endorsement of the need to track down the Munich criminals.

The film was not hugely successful, but it did all right, with a total worldwide box office in the range of $130 million. It received mixed reviews, but achieved Oscar nominations for best picture, best director, and best adapted screenplay. I don't think Spielberg was particularly hurt by this reception, though he perhaps did not receive due credit for the earnestness and honorableness of his humanistic message, for the fact that he had introduced, on the largest possible stage (or screen), a new factor in the endless, largely circular, and frequently bloody development of Israeli–Palestinian relations.

The movie remains underrated in Spielberg's body of work. Most of his films either carry no great moral or present an obvious one. There can be no question about the terrible meaning of *Schindler's List*. Or for that matter what the enslaved protagonists of *Amistad* should represent to us.

"**I certainly tried to bring an early 70s Hollywood style, a *cinéma vérité* style, with zoom lenses, and tools that we used to make those movies — one of my favorites being *The Day of the Jackal*.**"

But *Munich* is a different proposition altogether. There can be no question, as Spielberg says, that the murderers of the Olympians had to be tracked down and killed. To have done otherwise would have been irrevocably to weaken Israel's position in the endless and bloody tumult of the Middle East.

But to raise the question of the human cost of that activity, to point out the need somehow, sometime, to move beyond the eye-for-an-eye syndrome, presents a more nuanced position. "A response to a response is a never-ending cycle that doesn't really solve anything. It just creates a perpetual-motion machine. I never tried to answer the question of Israeli policy. That's not up to me. I'm not a diplomat. I'm not a politician. I'm a filmmaker, not a policy maker, so I didn't give answers. But I think the movie has a searching spirit and it asks a lot of questions."

Yes, it does, and they were questions that were not being asked at the time, or since, in forums as public as the movies—especially movies that must, perforce, aspire to audiences as large as this one had to attract if it was to succeed. Spielberg, speaking in the early days after *Munich*'s release, liked to quote a couple of sentences from the Israeli writer Amos Oz: "In the lives of individuals, and of peoples, too, the worst conflicts are often those that break out between those that are persecuted. Often each sees in the other not a partner in misfortune, but, in fact, the image of their common oppressor." Spielberg says he was haunted by those lines the whole time he was making his movie.

On location outside the Hungarian State Opera House, Budapest. In order to get the movie ready for a Christmas release for Oscar consideration, all of the scenes in Malta and Hungary were edited on the spot. The Paris and New York scenes were edited two weeks after photography and the final cut was readied after another two weeks.

INDIANA JONES

AND THE KINGDOM OF

THE

CRYSTAL

SKULL

(2008)

"I'm very obedient to the stories that George writes. I'll fight things I don't believe in, but ultimately, if George wants to bring interdimensional beings into *Crystal Skull,* I will do the best job I possibly can to acquit his idea and make him proud."

Steven Spielberg and George Lucas fell into a minor squabble about the plot of *Indiana Jones and the Kingdom of the Crystal Skull*. There was, of course, this lost city in South America to which one eponymous skull must be restored, and a villainous Russian agent (Cate Blanchett no less, out for a good time and having one), who believes the skull has mystical powers that can have Cold War uses (the time is 1957 and hints of McCarthyism occasionally, not too persuasively, dog Indy's tracks). Along the way we happily encounter Karen Allen as Marion, Indy's long-lost love, and Shia LaBeouf as Mutt Williams, who turns out, unsurprisingly, to be Indy's unacknowledged son with Marion.

This time Indy is joined by eager-beaver Mutt Williams (Shia LaBeouf), with whom he turns out to have more in common than just a love of adventure.

There is a kind of reunion air about the thing, which doesn't in any way interfere with the action—including a spectacular car chase that is top-of-the-line Spielberg.

In all, the picture is a pretty snappy sequel—especially as it was released 27 years after the first Indiana Jones picture appeared and most of the creative talent involved were now in their sixties. There is no letup in its creative energy. What got Spielberg's goat was Lucas's notion that the hidden South American city was founded by aliens from outer space; he thought the idea was superfluous, and his "best friend" did not.

They wrangled about it for a while without losing their tempers—until Spielberg surrendered. He thought: What the heck, George for some reason was committed to the idea and it did not materially affect the rationale for the movie's main line of business, which was to get everyone running around in perilous, but never really life-threatening, action. Spielberg was heard to say that he really had no option. If his pal of several decades wanted aliens, then, by God, let's give him aliens.

Harrison Ford was one of the 60-somethings by this time, and occasionally threatening retirement. But he's as spry as a cricket in this film. There's not a lot of evidence of stunt doubles in this performance, though there is, I think, a kind of wistfulness in his work—fewer wisecracks,

for example (though he is, as ever, terrified of snakes), and a kind of live-and-let-live attitude toward all and sundry as he pursues his quest. He's tolerant of the eager-beaver LaBeouf, even kind of mentoring in his gruff way, and he's more than glad to see Karen Allen again. It is one of the delights of this movie that, finally, after decades of separation, the pair are united, till death do them part, at the end of the film.

The best thing about *Crystal Skull*—which seems to me a little darker in tone than the previous Indy pictures, not quite so insouciant—is that nobody is just going through the motions as they pursue their more-than-agreeable pay packets. It has always seemed to me that, in serious or non-serious mode, Ford gives full value in his movies. He's never just finger-painting. We've had reason to observe that he thinks long and hard about his films before committing to them, and that when he does he throws himself into them with a full heart. And he is receptive to good, goofy ideas. For some reason, I think of Indy escaping harm from an atomic blast by tucking himself uncomfortably into a refrigerator. It's a silly, humorous, slightly horrific sequence that's almost thrown away. But it is also a sign, as if any were needed, that Spielberg is ever an alert filmmaker (think again about that flaming train in *War of the Worlds*).

With the action moving forward to the mid-1950s, the Nazis of the earlier films have been replaced by Cold War agents, and artillery fire by atomic test projects. At the age of 65, Harrison Ford has no need to rope in a stunt double (opposite, center). Owing to safety improvements, he was able to perform many of his own stunts, which he felt improved his performance.

"I was sort of amazed that all of us got our Indy legs back in the first couple of days of shooting, and that was the good news. It was a real reunion, with the sweetest memories."

The reviewers were good-natured about the finished product. Here and there they grumbled about Spielberg reverting to a type of movie they thought he had long since put behind him, though one of them reminded her readers that "Spielberg," literally translated from the German, means "play mountain." As we've had occasion to observe before, playfulness is a vital element of his gift. He would be at least a little bit lost without it. *Schindler's List*, yes. *Lincoln*, yes. But without occasionally giving vent to his talent for inconsequential, bravura filmmaking, he would be a lesser director. He needs, in short, to stay in touch with his roots.

The film premiered at Cannes—out of competition, of course—and it was well received, as it was throughout the world in the immediate aftermath of that event. Some observed—or thought they observed—that *Crystal Skull* was a little less rapturously talked about in the aftermath of its two hours on screen than it was in its excited anticipation. But that was not necessarily a provable point. As Spielberg sailed away on a yacht for a couple of weeks' rest and recuperation, his picture was poised for a worldwide gross, on first release, in excess of $780 million. The money was agreeable, of course, but by this time in his career, it didn't mean anything, practically speaking. It was just a means of quantifying success, not a way of fulfilling any conceivable material need that might yet be frustrating him.

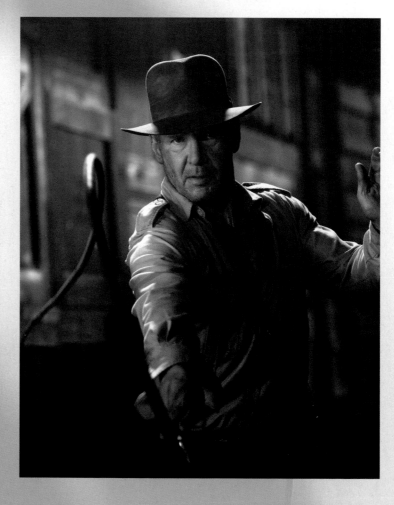

Possibly for the last time Harrison Ford cracks the whip. Paramount executives wanted the weapon to be computer generated to meet film safety rules, but the actor insisted on handling the real thing.

"In 1989 I thought the curtain was lowering on the series, which is why I had all the characters literally ride off into the sunset at the end. But ever since then, the most common question I get asked, all over the world, is: 'When are you going to make another *Indiana Jones*?'"

THE ADVENTURES OF TINTIN
THE SECRET OF THE UNICORN

(2011)

"Even though it was 28 years in my heart, two years of prep, and three physical years making this film, this was the most fun I've had since *E.T.*"

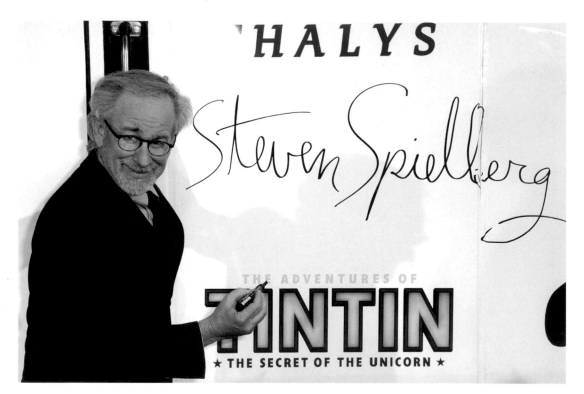

Shortly after *Raiders of the Lost Ark* opened in France, Spielberg was applying his "C-minus" high-school French to the task of reading some of the Parisian reviews of the film. In one of them he noticed a comparison of Harrison Ford's character to Tintin, hero of the series of comic books written and illustrated by the Belgian artist Hergé. He was curious enough to have the review translated and to obtain a couple of the Tintin books, in which he saw that the eponymous leading character (always accompanied by Snowy, his brave and loyal terrier) was at the very least a first cousin to Indiana Jones in his improbable, far-darting adventurousness.

The principal difference between them was that Tintin was a boy journalist, while Jones was, of course, an adult archaeologist.

"It stood on its own two legs for me," Spielberg says. Tintin had another partner in his adventures, a reprobate character named Captain Archibald Haddock, but most important was that the books had "furor, and there was suspense and there was action and there was a beautiful color palette." He spoke to Hergé on the phone, with the idea of having a meeting with him the next time Spielberg was in France. The artist was very excited about this prospect—he was a great movie fan and his work was heavily influenced by the silent film comedians.

That meeting did not take place because Hergé died in 1983. But his widow, Fanny, invited Spielberg and Kathy Kennedy to meet with her when they were in Europe making scenes for *Indiana Jones and the Temple of Doom*. Shortly thereafter, he optioned the rights to make a movie out of Tintin. There, however, the project languished. Spielberg could not get a script that he liked and after some 10 years he dropped his option.

This did not betoken a loss of interest on Spielberg's part, and sometime around 2001 he inquired again about the Tintin rights, which were still available, and he re-optioned them with an eye to making the film that eventually appeared in the fall season of 2011. As it happens, that is almost 28 years since Spielberg first expressed interest in Tintin—"my house record from the first time I optioned the rights."

Some things had changed over the years. The film is in 3-D. And, more important, it makes use of the relatively new "performance-capture" technology, which was irresistible to the techno-forward Spielberg. It is not straightforward to explain, but, in essence, it involves translating the movements of real-life actors into 2-D or 3-D computer-animated figures.

The process unfolds on what is called a "volume"— a white-and-gray stage with a hundred or more cameras hanging from a ceiling grid and focusing on the real-life actors as they go through their paces. All of the players' outfits are equipped with reflective dots near each joint, with each dot individually tracked by the cameras.

Checking the script with producer Peter Jackson, himself the director of the hugely successful *Lord of the Rings* trilogy. The pair first worked together on *The Lovely Bones* in 2009, with Jackson as director and Spielberg as executive producer. Spielberg's customary baseball cap is traded for a bowler as he and Jackson improvise as the bumbling detectives Thomson and Thompson (above, right), played in the movie by Simon Pegg and Nick Frost.

Overleaf: Before and after—capturing the motion of Jamie Bell and Andy Serkis as Tintin and Captain Haddock (left-hand page) leads to spectacular results (right-hand page).

"I'm flattered when *Tintin* is compared to *Raiders*, but I took no special measures to enhance the comparisons."

This provides skeletal images of the actors as well as rendering their most subtle facial expressions (captured by small, helmet-mounted cameras). The film's sets and props are also rendered digitally.

This material—there are over 1,200 shots in the film—was then turned over to animators, who provided volume, mass and, above all, expression to everyone, over a period of some 18 months. Peter Jackson, the director of *The Lord of the Rings* trilogy, was a significant collaborator with Spielberg throughout this painstaking process and both men were, if anything, more pleased with the results than they had anticipated.

As they had the right to be. *Tintin* renders Hergé's striking drawings with what seems to me perfect fidelity. Indeed, Spielberg was heard to murmur that the performance-capture process enabled him, at times, to move the action at more than lifelike speed, something he could not, of course, do with performers tethered to what the human body can realistically accomplish in real time.

And there is a lot of action in *Tintin*. It is, in fact, a tour de force in that regard. Spielberg had created individual sequences in many other films that approach what he virtuosically accomplishes here. But none of those movies comes close to this film, which is all non-stop, wall-to-wall activity, involving purloined treasure maps, bumbling

Spielberg has succeeded in capturing the "furor, suspense, action, and beautiful color palette" he so admired in Hergé's original books, with a touch of Indiana Jones added in.

detectives, a snarky villain, and, of course, Tintin and Snowy and the cranky Captain Haddock in more or less constant, if often comical, peril.

This question naturally arises: Is it all a little too much? A little too breathless? We need in films of this kind, some moments to step back, take stock, just plain relax before we hurry on to more derring-do. One thinks, it's a little too cartoonish. And then one remembers: It *is* a cartoon. And, all things considered, rather a bold one—if only for its brilliant use of motion capture.

Put simply, *The Adventures of Tintin* captivates children because its broad-stroke action will read clearly to them at almost any age they encounter it. Their accompanying parents and guardians will just have to live with its rather slapdash characterizations and its sometimes manic haste, for, in any case, they are bound to be wowed by the sheer expertise of its production, which, at times, raises the state of the art to the state of art as it is more generally defined.

I don't particularly "like" *Tintin*. That is to say, I think that it sacrifices warmth and good humor to its manic emphasis on non-stop action. But, by the same token, you have to acknowledge the raw power of its technology. It is truly at the forefront of motion capture. It is not *the* wave of the future. But is *a* wave of things to come. And in today's movie world that is no small achievement.

WAR HORSE

(2011)

"Every time I delve into an episode of history that I don't know very much about, my first reaction is anger that my teachers never taught me about it."

The talk about the hugely successful theatrical adaptation of Michael Morpurgo's novel for children *War Horse* was largely about the puppets—life-sized skeletal representations of horses manipulated by visible puppeteers so as to uncannily imitate the movements and attitudes of the equines as they acted out the fate, grim but ultimately triumphant, of a horse named Joey, a noble beast who is sold into the British army in World War I, and endures the hell of trench warfare on the Western Front.

"This is a human narrative. It's about the connectivity that an animal can bring to human characters. It's really much more of a story of hope and the hope that actually can exist in extremely dark circumstances."

According to Spielberg, the movie "just got on a fast track that was a little bit like a runaway horse. And I was hanging to the mane ..."

Cinematographer Janusz Kaminski's rendering of the glories of the Devonshire countryside and the horrors of trench warfare is one of the great strengths of *War Horse*.

This was a *coup de théâtre* of the first order—at first glance. After a time, however, this horsing around began to pale. Or so it seemed to me. More and more, as the evening wore on, the puppets (particularly Joey) came to seem a distraction from the essential simplicity of the story, which has a poverty-stricken farmer foolishly over-paying for the horse, who is trained by his son Albert, who forges an unshakable bond with the animal. When war comes, the animal is sold to the army and Albert spends the rest of the film searching for him in the trenches. Boy gets horse, boy loses horse, boy regains horse.

The play was seen in London by Stacey Snider, principal partner and co-chairman of DreamWorks, and by Kathleen Kennedy, who reported enthusiastically about its movie possibilities to Spielberg and ordered him to buy it, sight unseen. The deal was still being negotiated when Spielberg and his wife arrived in London to see the show, which he greatly enjoyed.

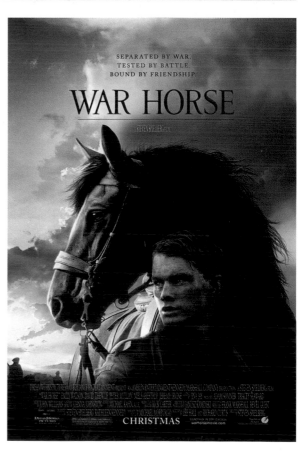

There was no question of carrying the puppet device over into the film version. The movie would have to be, as most movies are, an exercise in romantic realism, which was all right with Spielberg. He had thought his next film would be *Lincoln*, which was almost, but not quite, ready to budget and send out to actors. *War Horse*, on the other hand, was closer to being ready—it was just a question of adapting a well-structured play to the screen, which Lee Hall and, latterly, Richard Curtis speedily accomplished. "The fact that I was seeing a story that was so strong and so powerful is what attracted me to it," Spielberg says, "—just the human-interest element to the story and my other interest in epic wartime stories. The puppets became irrelevant."

So, "it just got on a fast track that was a little bit like a runaway horse. And I was hanging to the mane because there were no reins on this horse."

In adapting the piece for film, it is clearly necessary to rely entirely on the strength of the story—and the power of romantic realism—to sustain our interest, and I was not at all certain that *War Horse* would have that force. But it does. That's because Spielberg maintains a powerful tension between the pastoral and the battlefield action. The end result, to me at least, is a surprisingly powerful film. It is, structurally, intrinsically, a sentimental film. There is no getting around that. But Spielberg backs off from those

elements of the story, keeps his distance from them. To a very large degree he trusts the tale, rich in horrific incident, but full of grace notes as well, to tell itself with great simplicity.

In part, it also explores territory that is new to him. That is the pastoral. In the lengthy opening section of the film, the Devonshire countryside is presented in idyllic form. It is almost heartbreakingly beautiful. The farm is in constant jeopardy from the rich realtor who holds the paper on it, but Albert—nicely played in the film by Jeremy Irvine, with a fine blend of innocence and single-mindedness—and his parents, with a notably limpid performance by Emily Watson as his patient mother, are portrayed with great strength.

The horse, the boy, the growing bond between them, are presented with unfailing, but unpretentious, handsomeness. This is the world as it should be, and the contrast between it and the horrors of war, which preoccupy most of the rest of the film, lingers movingly in our minds. The war scenes take us into territory that is more familiar to Spielberg, though I must say the sheer terror that Joey endures at the front has rarely been rendered with the power he achieves here. The animal becomes a kind of wild thing, frightened yet brave and, admittedly, very lucky to survive more than a few minutes, let alone some four years. Indeed, the war

Previous pages: As Albert, Jeremy Irvine combined innocence and determination in his search for Joey (top, first three photos). "Be brave!" Benedict Cumberbatch, Patrick Kennedy, and Tom Hiddleston move forward to lead the doomed charge into the enemy camp (top, far right).

lasts so long that Albert ends up serving in it and spending much of his time searching for the beloved creature.

Spielberg makes it sound as if *War Horse* was a kind of godsend. As I think it was. There is a passion about it that, I think, surprised even him. And those puppets will largely be forgotten by the world audience for the film, to whom, frankly, they are no more than a distant rumor.

Meantime, we have this puppetless movie to deal with. I think, as I have surely implied, that it is a stronger movie than I bargained for. It profits from its realistic air, which encompasses both tenderness and terror, and is driven by Spielberg's typically relentless pacing. Even the sharp break between its pastoral beginnings and its scenes of trench warfare is ridden over—without hesitation. We are in one place; then we are in another, very different place. We gather from this movie what seems to me, at least, an uncommon passion for its subject matter. This is not to say that Spielberg ever makes a movie that does not enlist his full commitment. But there is, I think, something—well, different—about *War Horse*, which is inexplicable to the outsider. And, perhaps, to Spielberg himself. Though he makes a try.

"You know, if I stay very active I have a better grasp on my life and my work—if there aren't too many rest stops where I get a chance to think something through. My worst enemy is spending too much time thinking and my greatest ally is just jumping into the fray. Everything that I have spent too much time pondering I wind up not making. If I spend too much time on one project without any respite or any chance to reload my energy cells or simply to take a break and come back to it fresh, it stales quickly. I can't do that if all I have in front of me is *Lincoln* or a dinosaur or an *E.T.* I need other things in my life, both my personal life and my work life."

The congruence of *Tintin* and *War Horse*, released within days of each other in the United States, offers a perfect example of a situation Spielberg likes best. One is a project he nursed along for almost three decades, the other is something that blew into his life very quickly; one is a light-minded, yet technically venturesome movie, the other is a sober, traditional sort of film; one appeals to the perpetual child in him, the other calls out to the cultural striver in him. "Can't I be both?" Spielberg once plaintively asked.

The answer is, of course he can—though that gift of range (and ambition) is one that has been vouchsafed to few, if any, filmmakers either now or in the past. I think, more than any other quality, it defines his gift. And I think it is very odd of critics who have written about him to ignore his protean qualities. They are too bedazzled by his multi-layered success to notice that this restlessness is the very essence of the man.

Fast Forward

As this is written, *Lincoln* is in post-production and is due for release in December, 2012. It is based on the Pulitzer Prize-winning book *Team of Rivals* by Doris Kearns Goodwin, and starring Daniel Day-Lewis, with a script, once again, by Tony Kushner. Abraham Lincoln is, by all accounts, his longest-running obsession, dating back to childhood.

He was seven or eight years old when one of his uncles took him on a trip with his own son to Washington, D.C. to visit the historical sights. The one that impressed him the most was the Lincoln Memorial, which frightened him. "I was very little and Lincoln was very big, sitting on that throne, that great chair. I was very intimidated by it and almost couldn't make eye contact with the figurehead of Lincoln."

That, however, didn't stop him from reading about Lincoln. "I was dyslexic I now know—I didn't then—but as I started reading I would always read better when Lincoln was in the material than I would if it was just a science exercise in school." He adds: "I've done everything except buy a Lincoln—I have everything but the car. I've read the books, seen the documentaries." Then, in 1999, he encountered the author Doris Kearns Goodwin, and asked her what she was going to do next. She said that she was thinking of writing a book about Lincoln's presidency, to which Spielberg replied, "I'll buy it." She said she hadn't even found a publisher for the work, to which he responded, "I don't care. I'll buy it from you now and when you find a publisher just tell them that you've already given the film rights over to me and DreamWorks," which is exactly what happened.

"I'm like a kid whose eyes are bigger than his stomach. There are so many movies I want to make. I used to sit around wondering why nobody would make a movie about this subject or that. Now I can make those missing movies myself."

"Why would anybody stop doing this?" Spielberg's lifelong love affair with the cinema shows no sign of abating, although these days he prefers a more comfortable seat than when pedaling around the MGM Studios, 1982, while producing *Poltergeist*.

Over the years, Spielberg commissioned a number of scripts, none of which seemed to him tightly enough focused on the aspects of Lincoln's character that most interested him. It was only after he turned the writing job over to Kushner that he began to hear Lincoln's voice—and those of his "team of rivals" as well. Not that Kushner's work was exactly trim; his first draft ran to some 550 pages—a typical screenplay is usually about 120 pages long.

There was a passage in it, however, that resonated with Spielberg. It involved the passing of the Constitution's thirteenth amendment, which abolished slavery, and the ending of the Civil War—in other words, events that took place during the last months of Lincoln's life. It was on this part of the draft that Spielberg asked Kushner to focus, resulting in a final screenplay of around 150 pages, about two and a half hours of screen time.

By this time Spielberg will have completed principal photography on an utterly different sort of film, *Robopocalypse*, a science-fiction story about the aftermath of a robot revolt in some future time. And after that ...?

No one knows, including, so far as I can determine, Steven Spielberg.

He is now 65 years old and eligible, preposterous as that sounds, for Social Security in the United States. Considering that I have seen estimates of his net worth at approximately three billion dollars, it seems unlikely that he will be applying for government largesse any time soon.

He is, moreover, in good health and ebullient spirits. He thinks, sometimes, about his friend Clint Eastwood making ever better movies at the age of 82 and aspires to a similar late-life fecundity. "That would be a dream come true if it happens." He pauses to think: "You know, it's just ... Why would anybody stop doing this?"

Why, indeed? If he did suddenly stop, he would have to his credit at least a half-dozen films that will, I think, remain unforgettable: *Jaws*, *E.T.*, *Empire of the Sun*, *Jurassic Park*, *Schindler's List*, *Saving Private Ryan*, and a handful of other entertainments that people will resort to as long as they look to expertly made movies as a source of good times. Moreover, these films have a range of subject matter that is wider than that of any director one can conveniently cite. They also have certain thematic consistencies (communication, lost boys, and so on) that are well enough hidden not to be distracting, but obvious enough if one thinks even superficially about his body of work.

He is, if anything, too successful. We like our artists to have their struggles. He has not had many of those—if any. He is also too rich, and has been from the time, at least, of *Jaws*. These factors obscure the essential seriousness of his work and its enormous technical facility. A few misfires cannot dim these accomplishments.

If this book has a theme, it is that Spielberg's success hides his seriousness of purpose. He is, I think, too much taken for granted, too omnipresent. He has everything. Including the world's affection and respect—and a fair share of its awards as well. He has nothing more to prove to anyone. Except, of course, to himself. There will always be, for him, one more irresistible film to make. Or so one confidently imagines.

Heels over head. Steven Spielberg and Kate Capshaw, married since 1991, have traveled far together since that Shanghai nightclub scene in *Indiana Jones and the Temple of Doom*.

"My two great loves are family and making movies. Balancing the two is life's biggest challenge."

The director as portrayed by Chris Guise
of Weta Workshop, which conceptualized
The Adventures of Tintin.

Filmography

As Director

Amateur films

The Last Gun
8 minutes
Screenplay: Steven Spielberg
Cinematographer: Steven Spielberg
Cast: Steven Spielberg
1959

Fighter Squad
8 minutes
Screenplay: Steven Spielberg
Cinematographer: Steven Spielberg
Cast: Steven Spielberg
1961

Escape to Nowhere
40 minutes
Screenplay: Steven Spielberg
Cinematographer: Steven Spielberg
Cast: Anne Spielberg
1961

Firelight
140 minutes
Screenplay: Steven Spielberg
Cinematographer: Steven Spielberg
Cast: Robert Robyn, Beth Weber,
Lucky Lohr, Margaret Peyou
Opened March 24, 1964

Slipstream
Unfinished
Screenplay: Steven Spielberg,
Roger Ernest
Cinematographer: Serge Haignere
Cast: Jim Baxes, Tony Bill, Roger
Ernest, Peter Maffia, Andre Oviedo
1967

Amblin'
26 minutes
Screenplay: Steven Spielberg
Cinematographer: Allen Daviau
Cast: Richard Levin, Pamela McMyler
Opened December 18, 1968

Feature films

*Note: Opening dates are for the USA
(general release) unless stated.*

Duel
(Universal Television)
90 minutes (theatrical version),
74 minutes (TV version)
Screenplay: Richard Matheson
Cinematographer: Jack A. Marta
Cast: Dennis Weaver (David Mann),
Eddie Firestone (café owner), Gene
Dynarski (man in café)
TV version first broadcast November
10, 1971 (Canada); theatrical version
opened March 21, 1973 (Europe)

The Sugarland Express
(Universal/Zanuck-Brown)
110 minutes
Screenplay: Hal Barwood,
Matthew Robbins
Cinematographer: Vilmos Zsigmond
Cast: Goldie Hawn (Lou Jean Poplin),
Ben Johnson (Captain Harlin
Tanner), Michael Sacks (Patrolman
Maxwell Slide), William Atherton
(Clovis Michael Poplin), Gregory
Walcott (Patrolman Ernie Mashburn)
Opened April 5, 1974

Jaws
(Universal/Zanuck-Brown)
124 minutes
Screenplay: Carl Gottlieb,
Peter Benchley
Cinematographer: Bill Butler
Cast: Roy Scheider (Martin
Brody), Robert Shaw (Sam Quint),
Richard Dreyfuss (Matt Hooper),
Lorraine Gary (Ellen Brody),
Murray Hamilton (Mayor Vaughn),
Jeffrey Kramer (Hendricks)
Opened June 20, 1975

**Close Encounters of the Third
Kind**
(Columbia/EMI)
135 minutes
Screenplay: Steven Spielberg
Cinematographer: Vilmos Zsigmond
Cast: Richard Dreyfuss (Roy Neary),
François Truffaut (Claude Lacombe),
Teri Garr (Ronnie Neary), Melinda
Dillon (Jillian Guiler), Bob Balaban
(David Laughlin)
Opened November 16, 1977

1941
(Universal/Columbia/A-Team)
118 minutes
Screenplay: Robert Zemeckis,
Bob Gale
Cinematographer: William A. Fraker
Cast: Dan Aykroyd (Sgt. Frank Tree),
Ned Beatty (Ward Douglas), John
Belushi (Capt. Wild Bill Kelso),
Lorraine Gary (Joan Douglas),
Murray Hamilton (Claude Crumm),
Christopher Lee (Capt. Wolfgang
von Kleinschmidt), Tim Matheson
(Capt. Loomis Birkhead), Toshiro
Mifune (Cmdr. Akiro Mitamura),
Warren Oates (Col. "Madman"
Maddox), Robert Stack (Maj. Gen.
Joseph W. Stilwell)
Opened December 14, 1979

Raiders of the Lost Ark
(Paramount/Lucasfilm)
115 minutes
Screenplay: Lawrence Kasdan
Cinematographer: Douglas Slocombe
Cast: Harrison Ford (Indiana Jones),
Karen Allen (Marion Ravenwood),
Paul Freeman (Dr. René Belloq),
Ronald Lacey (Major Arnold Toht),
John Rhys-Davies (Sallah),
Denholm Elliott (Dr. Marcus Brody)
Opened June 14, 1981

E.T.: The Extra-Terrestrial
(Universal)
115 minutes
Screenplay: Melissa Mathison
Cinematographer: Allen Daviau
Cast: Dee Wallace (Mary), Henry
Thomas (Elliott), Peter Coyote
(Keys), Robert MacNaughton
(Michael), Drew Barrymore (Gertie),
K.C. Martel (Greg), Sean Frye (Steve)
Opened June 11, 1982

Twilight Zone: The Movie
(anthology film with segments
directed by John Landis, Spielberg,
Joe Dante, and George Miller)
(Warner Bros.)
101 minutes
Spielberg segment: "Kick the Can"
Screenplay: George Clayton Johnson,
Richard Matheson, Melinda Mathison
(as Josh Rogan)
Cinematographer: Allen Daviau
Cast: Scatman Crothers (Mr. Bloom),
Bill Quinn (Mr. Conroy),
Martin Garner (Mr. Weinstein),
Selma Diamond (Mrs. Weinstein),
Helen Shaw (Mrs. Dempsey)
Opened June 24, 1983

**Indiana Jones and the Temple
of Doom**
(Paramount/Lucasfilm)
118 minutes
Screenplay: Willard Huyck,
Gloria Katz
Cinematographer: Douglas Slocombe
Cast: Harrison Ford (Indiana Jones),
Kate Capshaw (Willie Scott),
Ke Huy Quan (Short Round),
Amrish Puri (Mola Ram),
Rushan Seth (Chattar Lal),
Philip Stone (Blumburtt)
Opened May 23, 1984

The Color Purple
(Amblin/Guber-Peters/
Warner Bros.)
154 minutes
Screenplay: Menno Meyjes
Cinematographer: Allen Daviau
Cast: Danny Glover (Albert), Whoopi
Goldberg (Celie), Margaret Avery
(Shug), Oprah Winfrey (Sofia),
Willard Pugh (Harpo)
Opened December 22, 1985

Empire of the Sun
(Amblin/Warner Bros.)
152 minutes
Screenplay: Tom Stoppard
Cinematographer: Allen Daviau
Cast: Christian Bale (Jim "Jamie"
Graham), John Malkovich (Basie),
Miranda Richardson (Mrs. Victor),
Nigel Havers (Dr. Rawlins),
Joe Pantoliano (Frank Demarest),
Leslie Phillips (Maxton)
Opened December 13, 1987

**Indiana Jones and the
Last Crusade**
(Paramount/Lucasfilm)
127 minutes
Screenplay: Jeffrey Boam
Cinematographer: Douglas Slocombe
Cast: Harrison Ford (Indiana Jones),
Sean Connery (Professor Henry
Jones), Denholm Elliott
(Dr. Marcus Brody), Alison Doody
(Dr. Elsa Schneider), John Rhys-
Davies (Sallah), Julian Glover
(Walter Donovan), River Phoenix
(young Indy)
Opened May 24, 1989

Always
(Amblin/United Artists/Universal)
122 minutes
Screenplay: Jerry Belson
Cinematographer: Mikael Salomon
Cast: Richard Dreyfuss (Pete
Sandich), Holly Hunter (Dorinda
Durston), Brad Johnson (Ted Baker),
John Goodman (Al Yackey),
Audrey Hepburn (Hap)
Opened December 22, 1989

Hook
(Amblin/TriStar)
144 minutes
Screenplay: Jim V. Hart,
Malia Scotch Marmo
Cinematographer: Dean Cundey
Cast: Dustin Hoffman (Capt. Hook),
Robin Williams (Peter Banning),
Julia Roberts (Tinkerbell),
Bob Hoskins (Smee), Maggie Smith
(Granny Wendy)
Opened December 15, 1991

Jurassic Park
(Universal/Amblin)
127 minutes
Screenplay: Michael Crichton,
David Koepp
Cinematographer: Dean Cundey
Cast: Sam Neill (Dr. Alan Grant),
Laura Dern (Dr. Ellie Sattler),
Jeff Goldblum (Dr. Ian Malcolm),
Richard Attenborough
(John Hammond), Bob Peck
(Robert Muldoon)
Opened June 13, 1993

Schindler's List
(Universal/Amblin)
195 minutes
Screenplay: Steven Zaillian
Cinematographer: Janusz Kaminski
Cast: Liam Neeson (Oskar Schindler),
Ben Kingsley (Itzhak Stern), Ralph
Fiennes (Amon Goeth), Caroline
Goodall (Emilie Schindler)
Opened December 17, 1993

The Lost World: Jurassic Park
(Universal/Amblin)
129 minutes
Screenplay: David Koepp
Cinematographer: Janusz Kaminski
Cast: Jeff Goldblum (Dr. Ian
Malcolm), Julianne Moore (Dr. Sarah
Harding), Pete Postlethwaite (Roland
Tembo), Richard Attenborough
(John Hammond)
Opened May 27, 1997

Amistad
(DreamWorks/HBO)
155 minutes
Screenplay: David Franzoni
Cinematographer: Janusz Kaminski
Cast: Morgan Freeman (Theodore
Joadson), Nigel Hawthorne (Martin
Van Buren), Anthony Hopkins (John
Quincy Adams), Djimon Hounsou
(Cinquè), Matthew McConaughey
(Roger Sherman Baldwin)
Opened December 14, 1997

Saving Private Ryan
(Amblin/DreamWorks/
Mark Gordon Productions/Mutual
Film Company/Paramount)
169 minutes
Screenplay: Robert Rodat
Cinematographer: Janusz Kaminski
Cast: Tom Hanks (Capt. John H.
Miller), Tom Sizemore (Sgt. Mike
Horvath), Edward Burns (Pvt.
Richard Reiben), Barry Pepper
(Pvt. Daniel Jackson), Adam Goldberg
(Pvt. Stanley Mellish), Matt Damon
(Pvt. James Ryan), Ted Danson
(Capt. Fred Hamill)
Opened July 26, 1998

A.I.: Artificial Intelligence
(Warner Bros./DreamWorks/Amblin)
146 minutes
Screenplay: Steven Spielberg
Cinematographer: Janusz Kaminski
Cast: Haley Joel Osment (David),
Frances O'Connor (Monica Swinton),
Sam Robards (Henry Swinton), Jake
Thomas (Martin Swinton), Jude Law
(Gigolo Joe), William Hurt (Prof.
Hobby), Ken Leung (Syatyoo-Sama)
Opened July 1, 2001

Minority Report
(Twentieth Century Fox/
DreamWorks/Cruise-Wagner/
Blue Tulip Productions/Ronald
Shusett-Gary Goldman)
145 minutes
Screenplay: Scott Frank, Jon Cohen
Cinematographer: Janusz Kaminski
Cast: Tom Cruise (Chief John
Anderton), Max von Sydow (Director
Lamar Burgess), Steve Harris (Jad),
Neal McDonough (Fletcher), Patrick
Kilpatrick (Knott), Jessica Capshaw
(Evanna), Colin Farrell (Danny
Witwer), Samantha Morton (Agatha)
Opened June 21, 2002

Catch Me If You Can
(DreamWorks/Kemp Company/
Splendid Pictures/Parkes-
MacDonald/Muse)
141 minutes
Screenplay: Jeff Nathanson
Cinematographer: Janusz Kaminski
Cast: Leonardo DiCaprio (Frank
Abagnale, Jr.), Tom Hanks (Carl
Hanratty), Christopher Walken
(Frank Abagnale), Martin Sheen
(Roger Strong), Nathalie Baye
(Paula Abagnale), Amy Adams
(Brenda Strong)
Opened December 29, 2002

The Terminal
(DreamWorks/Amblin/
Parkes-MacDonald)
128 minutes
Screenplay: Sacha Gervasi,
Jeff Nathanson
Cinematographer: Janusz Kaminski
Cast: Tom Hanks (Viktor Navorski),
Catherine Zeta-Jones (Amelia
Warren), Stanley Tucci (Frank
Dixon), Chi McBride (Mulroy),
Diego Luna (Enrique Cruz)
Opened June 20, 2004

War of the Worlds
(Paramount/DreamWorks/Amblin/
Cruise-Wagner)
116 minutes
Screenplay: Josh Friedman,
David Koepp
Cinematographer: Janusz Kaminski
Cast: Tom Cruise (Ray Ferrier),
Dakota Fanning (Rachel Ferrier),
Miranda Otto (Mary Ann),
Justin Chatwin (Robbie), Tim
Robbins (Harlan Ogilvy), Rick
Gonzalez (Vincent)
Opened June 23, 2005

Munich
(DreamWorks/Universal/
Amblin/Kennedy-Marshall/
Barry Mendel Productions)
164 minutes
Screenplay: Tony Kushner, Eric Roth
Cinematographer: Janusz Kaminski
Cast: Eric Bana (Avner), Daniel Craig
(Steve), Ciarán Hinds (Carl), Mathieu
Kassovitz (Robert), Hanns Zischler
(Hans), Ayelet Zurer (Daphna),
Geoffrey Rush (Ephraim)
Opened December 23, 2005

**Indiana Jones and the Kingdom
of the Crystal Skull**
(Paramount/Lucasfilm)
122 minutes
Screenplay: David Koepp
Cinematographer: Janusz Kaminski
Cast: Harrison Ford (Indiana Jones),
Cate Blanchett (Irina Spalko),
Karen Allen (Marion Ravenwood),
Shia LaBeouf (Mutt Williams), Ray
Winstone ("Mac" George Michale),
John Hurt (Professor Oxley)
Opened May 25, 2008

**The Adventures of Tintin: The
Secret of the Unicorn**
(Paramount/Columbia/Amblin/
WingNut/Kennedy-Marshall)
107 minutes
Screenplay: Steven Moffatt, Edgar
Wright, Joe Cornish
Animation: Weta Workshop
Cast: Jamie Bell (Tintin),
Andy Serkis (Captain Haddock),
Daniel Craig (Ivanovich Sakharine),
Simon Pegg (Inspector Thompson),
Nick Frost (Inspector Thomson)
Opened December 21, 2011

War Horse
(DreamWorks/Reliance/Amblin/
Kennedy-Marshall)
146 minutes
Screenplay: Lee Hall, Richard Curtis
Cinematographer: Janusz Kaminski
Cast: Jeremy Irvine (Albert
Narracott), Emily Watson
(Rose Narracott), Peter Mullan
(Ted Narracott), David Thewlis
(Lyons), Benedict Cumberbatch
(Major Stewart)
Opened December 25, 2011

Lincoln
(Office Seekers/DreamWorks/
Amblin/Imagine/Kennedy-Marshall/
Parkes-MacDonald/Participant/
Reliance/Twentieth Century Fox)
Screenplay: Tony Kushner,
John Logan, Paul Webb
Cinematographer: Janusz Kaminski
Cast: Daniel Day-Lewis (Abraham
Lincoln), Joseph Gordon-Levitt
(Robert Todd Lincoln), Jared Harris
(Ulysses S. Grant), Tommy Lee Jones
(Thaddeus Stevens)
Opening December 2012

TV series

Night Gallery
(Universal Television)
2 episodes, 1969 (pilot)/1971

Marcus Welby, MD
(Universal Television)
1 episode, 1970

The Name of the Game
(Universal Television)
1 episode, 1971

The Psychiatrist
(Universal Television)
2 episodes, 1971

Owen Marshall: Counselor at Law
(Universal Television)
1 episode, 1971

Amazing Stories
(Amblin/Universal Television)
2 episodes, 1985

TV movies

**Mystery Movie:
Columbo: Murder by the Book**
(Universal Television)
76 minutes
Screenplay: Steven Bochco
Cinematographer: Russell Metty
Cast: Peter Falk (Lt. Columbo), Jack
Cassidy (Ken Franklin), Rosemary
Forsyth (Joanna Ferris)
First broadcast September 15, 1971

Duel (see page 279)

Something Evil
(Belford/CBS)
73 minutes
Screenplay: Robert Clouse
Cinematographer: Bill Butler
Cast: Sandy Dennis (Marjorie
Worden), Darren McGavin (Paul
Worden), Ralph Bellamy (Harry
Lincoln), Jeff Corey (Gehrmann)
First broadcast January 21, 1972

Savage
(Universal Television)
73 minutes
Screenplay: Richard Levinson,
William Link, Mark Rodgers
Cinematographer: Bill Butler
Cast: Martin Landau (Paul Savage),
Barbara Bain (Gail Abbott),
Will Geer (Joel Ryker)
First broadcast March 31, 1973

Documentaries

The Unfinished Journey
(CBS)
21 minutes
Screenplay: Tim Willocks
Cast: Maya Angelou, Bill Clinton,
Ossie Davis, Ruby Dee, Edward
James Olmos, Sam Waterston
(Themselves/Narrators)
First broadcast December 31, 1999

A Timeless Call
(Allentown/Jinks-Cohen)
7 minutes
Screenplay: Lorna Graham
Cast: Tom Hanks (Himself/Narrator),
Toby Meuli (Prom King)
First broadcast at the
Democratic National Convention,
August 25–28, 2008

As Producer

Feature films

Note: For films that Spielberg directed and produced, only producer details are listed here. See pages 271–272 for fuller details.

I Wanna Hold Your Hand
(Universal)
Director: Robert Zemeckis
Screenplay: Robert Zemeckis, Bob Gale
Producers: Tamara Asseyev, Alexandra Rose
Associate producer: Bob Gale
Executive producer: Steven Spielberg
Cast: Nancy Allen, Bobby Di Cicco, Mark McClure
Opened April 21, 1978

Used Cars
(Columbia/A-Team)
Director: Robert Zemeckis
Screenplay: Robert Zemeckis, Bob Gale
Producer: Bob Gale
Executive producers: John Milius, Steven Spielberg, John G. Wilson
Cast: Kurt Russell, Jack Warden, Gerrit Graham
Opened July 11, 1980

Continental Divide
(Universal/Amblin)
Director: Michael Apted
Screenplay: Lawrence Kasdan
Producer: Bob Larson
Associate producers: Zelda Barron, Jack Rosenthal
Executive producers: Bernie Brillstein, Steven Spielberg
Cast: John Belushi, Blair Brown, Allen Garfield
Opened September 18, 1981

E.T.: The Extra-Terrestrial
Producers: Kathleen Kennedy, Steven Spielberg
Associate producer: Melissa Mathison

Poltergeist
(MGM/SLM)
Director: Tobe Hooper
Screenplay: Steven Spielberg, Michael Grais, Mark Victor
Producers: Frank Marshall, Steven Spielberg
Associate producer: Kathleen Kennedy
Cast: JoBeth Williams, Heather O'Rourke, Craig T. Nelson
Opened June 4, 1982

Twilight Zone: The Movie
Producers: John Landis, Steven Spielberg
Associate producers: Jon Davison, Michael Finnell, Kathleen Kennedy
Executive producer: Frank Marshall
Producer (Spielberg-directed segment): Kathleen Kennedy

Gremlins
(Warner Bros./Amblin)
Director: Joe Dante
Screenplay: Chris Columbus
Producer: Michael Finnell
Executive producers: Kathleen Kennedy, Frank Marshall, Steven Spielberg
Cast: Zach Galligan, Phoebe Cates, Hoyt Axton
Opened June 8, 1984

Fandango
(Warner Bros./Amblin)
Director: Kevin Reynolds
Screenplay: Kevin Reynolds
Producer: Tim Zinnemann
Associate producers: Pat Kehoe, Barrie M. Osborne
Executive producers: Kathleen Kennedy, Frank Marshall, Steven Spielberg (uncredited)
Cast: Kevin Costner, Judd Nelson, Sam Robards
Opened January 25, 1985

The Goonies
(Warner Bros./Amblin)
Director: Richard Donner
Screenplay: Chris Columbus
Producers: Harvey Bernhard, Richard Donner
Executive producers: Kathleen Kennedy, Frank Marshall, Steven Spielberg
Cast: Sean Astin, Josh Brolin, Jeff Cohen
Opened June 7, 1985

Back to the Future
(Universal/Amblin/U-Drive [uncredited])
Director: Robert Zemeckis
Screenplay: Robert Zemeckis, Bob Gale
Producers: Neil Canton, Bob Gale
Executive producers: Kathleen Kennedy, Frank Marshall, Steven Spielberg
Cast: Michael J. Fox, Christopher Lloyd, Lea Thompson
Opened July 3, 1985

Young Sherlock Holmes
(Paramount/Amblin/ILM)
Director: Barry Levinson
Screenplay: Chris Columbus
Producers: Mark Johnson, Henry Winkler
Associate producer: Harry Benn
Executive producers: Kathleen Kennedy, Frank Marshall, Steven Spielberg
Cast: Nicholas Rowe, Alan Cox, Sophie Ward
Opened December 4, 1985

The Color Purple
Producers: Quincy Jones, Kathleen Kennedy, Frank Marshall, Steven Spielberg
Associate producer: Carol Isenberg
Executive producers: Peter Guber, Jon Peters

The Money Pit
(Universal/Amblin/U-Drive)
Director: Richard Benjamin
Screenplay: David Giler
Producers: Kathleen Kennedy, Art Levinson, Frank Marshall
Executive producers: David Giler, Steven Spielberg
Cast: Tom Hanks, Shelley Long, Alexander Godunov
Opened March 26, 1986

An American Tail
(Universal/Amblin/U-Drive/Sullivan)
Director: Don Bluth
Screenplay: Judy Freudberg, Tony Geiss
Producers: Don Bluth, Gary Goldman, John Pomeroy
Associate producers: Kate Barker, Deborah Jelin
Executive producers: Kathleen Kennedy, David Kirschner, Frank Marshall, Steven Spielberg
Cast: Dom DeLuise (voice), Christopher Plummer (voice), Erica Yohn (voice)
Opened November 21, 1986

Harry and the Hendersons (aka Bigfoot and the Hendersons)
(Universal/Amblin)
Director: William Dear
Screenplay: William Dear, William E. Martin, Ezra D. Rappaport
Producers: William Dear, Richard Vane
Associate producer: Frank Baur (uncredited)
Executive producer: Steven Spielberg (uncredited)
Cast: John Lithgow, Melinda Dillon, Margaret Langrick
Opened June 5, 1987

Innerspace
(Warner Bros./Amblin/Guber-Peters)
Director: Joe Dante
Screenplay: Jeffrey Boam, Chip Proser
Producer: Michael Finnell
Co-producer: Chip Proser
Executive producers: Peter Guber, Jon Peters, Steven Spielberg
Co-executive producers: Kathleen Kennedy, Frank Marshall
Cast: Dennis Quaid, Martin Short, Meg Ryan
Opened July 1, 1987

Three O'Clock High
(Universal)
Director: Phil Joanou
Screenplay: Richard Christian Matheson, Thomas E. Szollosi
Producer: David E. Vogel
Co-producers: John Davis, Neal Israel
Executive producers: Alan Greisman, Aaron Spelling, Steven Spielberg (uncredited)
Cast: Casey Siemaszko, Annie Ryan, Richard Tyson
Opened October 9, 1987

Empire of the Sun
Producers: Kathleen Kennedy, Frank Marshall, Steven Spielberg
Associate producer: Chris Kenny
Executive producer: Robert Shapiro

*batteries not included
(Universal/Amblin)
Director: Matthew Robbins
Screenplay: Brad Bird, Matthew Robbins, Brent Maddock, S.S. Wilson
Producer: Ronald L. Schwary
Associate producer: Gerald R. Molen
Executive producers: Kathleen Kennedy, Frank Marshall, Steven Spielberg
Cast: Hume Cronyn, Jessica Tandy, Frank McRae
Opened December 18, 1987

Who Framed Roger Rabbit
(Touchstone/Amblin/Silver Screen/Walt Disney [uncredited])
Director: Robert Zemeckis
Screenplay: Jeffrey Price, Peter S. Seaman
Producers: Frank Marshall, Robert Watts
Associate producers: Don Hahn, Steve Starkey
Executive producers: Kathleen Kennedy, Steven Spielberg
Cast: Bob Hoskins, Christopher Lloyd, Joanna Cassidy, Kathleen Turner (voice)
Opened June 22, 1988

The Land Before Time
(Universal/Amblin/Sullivan Bluth/U-Drive/Lucasfilm [uncredited])
Director: Don Bluth
Screenplay: Stu Krieger
Producers: Don Bluth, Gary Goldman, John Pomeroy
Associate producer: Deborah Jelin Newmyer
Executive producers: George Lucas, Steven Spielberg
Co-executive producers: Kathleen Kennedy, Frank Marshall
Cast: Pat Hingle (voice), Gabriel Damon (voice), Judith Barsi (voice)
Opened November 18, 1988

Dad
(Amblin/Ubu)
Director: Gary David Goldberg
Screenplay: Gary David Goldberg
Producers: Gary David Goldberg, Joseph Stern
Co-producers: Ric Kidney, Sam Weisman
Executive producers: Kathleen Kennedy, Frank Marshall, Steven Spielberg
Cast: Jack Lemmon, Ted Danson, Olympia Dukakis, Ethan Hawke
Opened October 27, 1989

Back to the Future Part II
(Universal/Amblin/U-Drive)
Director: Robert Zemeckis
Screenplay: Bob Gale
Producers: Neil Canton, Bob Gale
Associate producer: Steve Starkey
Executive producers: Kathleen
Kennedy, Frank Marshall,
Steven Spielberg
Cast: Michael J. Fox, Christopher
Lloyd, Lea Thompson,
Thomas F. Wilson
Opened November 22, 1989

Always
Producers: Kathleen Kennedy,
Frank Marshall, Steven Spielberg
Co-producer: Richard Vane

Joe Versus the Volcano
(Warner Bros./Amblin)
Director: John Patrick Shanley
Screenplay: John Patrick Shanley
Producer: Teri Schwartz
Associate producer: Roxanne Rogers
Executive producers: Kathleen
Kennedy, Frank Marshall,
Steven Spielberg
Cast: Tom Hanks, Meg Ryan,
Lloyd Bridges
Opened March 9, 1990

Back to the Future Part III
(Universal/Amblin/U-Drive)
Director: Robert Zemeckis
Screenplay: Bob Gale
Producers: Neil Canton, Bob Gale
Associate producer: Steve Starkey
Executive producers: Kathleen
Kennedy, Frank Marshall,
Steven Spielberg
Cast: Michael J. Fox, Christopher
Lloyd, Mary Steenburgen, Thomas
F. Wilson, Lea Thompson
Opened May 25, 1990

Gremlins 2: The New Batch
(Warner Bros./Amblin)
Director: Joe Dante
Screenplay: Charlie Haas
Producer: Michael Finnell
Co-producer: Rick Baker
Executive producers: Kathleen
Kennedy, Frank Marshall,
Steven Spielberg
Cast: Zach Galligan, Phoebe Cates,
John Glover
Opened June 15, 1990

Arachnophobia
(Hollywood/Amblin/Tangled Web)
Director: Frank Marshall
Screenplay: Don Jakoby,
Wesley Strick
Producers: Kathleen Kennedy,
Richard Vane
Co-producer: Don Jakoby
Associate producer:
William S. Beasley
Executive producers: Frank Marshall,
Steven Spielberg
Co-executive producers: Robert
W. Cort, Ted Field
Cast: Jeff Daniels, Julian Sands,
John Goodman
Opened July 19, 1990

Dreams
(aka Akira Kurosawa's Dreams)
(Warner Bros./Akira Kurosawa USA)
Directors: Akira Kurosawa,
Ishirô Honda
Screenplay: Akira Kurosawa
Producers: Mike Y. Inoue,
Hisao Kurosawa
Associate producers: Seikichi Iizumi,
Allan H. Liebert
Executive producer (international
version): Steven Spielberg
Cast: Akira Terao, Mitsuko Baishô,
Toshie Negishi
Opened August 24, 1990

Cape Fear
(Amblin/Cappa/Tribeca)
Director: Martin Scorsese
Screenplay: Wesley Strick
Producers: Barabara De Fina, Robert
De Niro (uncredited)
Executive producers: Kathleen
Kennedy, Frank Marshall, Steven
Spielberg (uncredited)
Cast: Robert De Niro, Nick Nolte,
Jessica Lange, Juliette Lewis
Opened November 13, 1991

An American Tail:
Fievel Goes West
(Universal/Amblin/Amblimation)
Directors: Phil Nibbelink,
Simon Wells
Screenplay: Flint Dille
Producers: Steven Spielberg,
Robert Watts
Associate producer: Stephen Hickner
Executive producers: Kathleen
Kennedy, David Kirschner,
Frank Marshall
Cast: Phillip Glasser (voice), James
Stewart (voice), Erica Yohn (voice),
Dom DeLuise (voice), Amy Irving
(voice), John Cleese (voice)
Opened November 22, 1991

We're Back! A Dinosaur's Story
(Universal/Amblin/Amblimation)
Directors: Phil Nibbelink, Simon
Wells, Dick Zondag, Ralph Zondag
Screenplay: John Patrick Shanley
Producer: Stephen Hickner
Co-producer: Thad Weinlein
Executive producers: Kathleen
Kennedy, Frank Marshall,
Steven Spielberg
Cast: John Goodman (voice),
Charles Fleischer (voice), Blaze
Berdahl (voice)
Opened November 24, 1993

Schindler's List
Producers: Branko Lustig, Gerald R.
Molen, Steven Spielberg
Co-producer: Lew Rywin
Associate producers: Irving Glovin,
Robert Raymond
Executive producer:
Kathleen Kennedy

The Flintstones
(Universal/Amblin/Hanna-Barbera)
Director: Brian Levant
Screenplay: Tom S. Parker, Jim
Jennewein, Steven E. de Souza
Producer: Bruce Cohen
Co-producer: Colin Wilson
Executive producers: Joseph Barbera,
William Hanna, Kathleen Kennedy,
David Kirschner, Gerald R. Molen,
Steven Spielberg (as Steven Spielrock)
Cast: John Goodman,
Elizabeth Perkins, Rick Moranis,
Rosie O'Donnell
Opened May 27, 1994

Casper
(Universal/Amblin/Harvey)
Director: Brad Silberling
Screenplay: Sherri Stoner,
Deanna Oliver
Producer: Colin Wilson
Co-producers: Jeff Franklin,
Steve Waterman
Associate producer: Paul Deason
Executive producers: Gerald R.
Molen, Jeffrey A. Montgomery,
Steven Spielberg
Cast: Bill Pullman, Christina Ricci,
Cathy Moriarty
Opened May 26, 1995

Balto
(Universal/Amblin/Amblimation)
Director: Simon Wells
Screenplay: David Steven Cohen,
Elana Lesser, Cliff Ruby,
Roger S.H. Schulman
Producer: Steven Hickner
Associate producer: Rich Arons
Executive producers: Kathleen
Kennedy, Bonne Radford,
Steven Spielberg
Cast: Kevin Bacon, Bob Hoskins,
Bridget Fonda
Opened December 22, 1995

Twister
(Warner Bros./Universal/Amblin/
Constant c)
Director: Jan de Bont
Screenplay: Michael Crichton,
Anne-Marie Martin
Producers: Ian Bryce, Michael
Crichton, Kathleen Kennedy
Associate producer: Glenn Salloum
Executive producers: Laurie
MacDonald, Gerald R. Molen, Walter
Parkes, Steven Spielberg
Cast: Helen Hunt, Bill Paxton,
Cary Elwes
Opened May 10, 1996

Men in Black
(Columbia/Amblin/
MacDonald-Parkes)
Director: Barry Sonnenfeld
Screenplay: Ed Solomon
Producers: Laurie MacDonald,
Walter Parkes
Co-producer: Graham Place
Associate producer: Steven R. Molen
Executive producer: Steven Spielberg
Cast: Tommy Lee Jones, Will Smith,
Linda Fiorentino
Opened July 2, 1997

Amistad
Producers: Debbie Allen, Steven
Spielberg, Colin Wilson
Co-producer: Tim Shriver
Associate producers: Bonnie Curtis,
Paul Deason
Executive producers: Laurie
MacDonald, Walter Parkes
Co-executive producer:
Robert Cooper

Deep Impact
(Paramount/DreamWorks/Zanuck-
Brown/Manhattan Project)
Director: Mimi Leder
Screenplay: Bruce Joel Rubin,
Michael Tolkin
Producers: David Brown,
Richard D. Zanuck
Associate producer: D. Scott Easton
Executive producers: Joan Bradshaw,
Walter Parkes, Steven Spielberg
Cast: Robert Duvall, Téa Leoni,
Elijah Wood, Vanessa Redgrave,
Morgan Freeman
Opened May 8, 1998

The Mask of Zorro
(TriStar/Amblin/David Foster/
Global/Zorro)
Director: Martin Campbell
Screenplay: John Eskow, Ted Elliott,
Terry Rossio
Producers: Doug Claybourne,
David Foster
Co-producer: John Gertz
Associate producer: Tava R. Maloy
Executive producers: Laurie
MacDonald, Walter Parkes,
Steven Spielberg
Cast: Antonio Banderas, Anthony
Hopkins, Catherine Zeta-Jones
Opened July 17, 1998

Saving Private Ryan
Producers: Ian Bryce, Mark Gordon,
Gary Levinsohn, Steven Spielberg
Co-producers: Bonnie Curtis, Allison
Lyon Segan
Associate producers: Kevin De La
Noy, Mark Huffam

The Haunting
(DreamWorks/Roth-Arnold)
Director: Jan de Bont
Screenplay: David Self
Producers: Susan Arnold, Donna
Arkoff Roth, Colin Wilson
Associate producer: Marty P. Ewing
Executive producers: Jan de Bont,
Samuel Z. Arkoff (uncredited),
Steven Spielberg (uncredited)
Cast: Liam Neeson, Catherine
Zeta-Jones, Owen Wilson
Opened July 23, 1999

Shrek
(DreamWorks Animation/
DreamWorks/PDI)
Directors: Andrew Adamson,
Vicky Jenson
Screenplay: Ted Elliott, Terry Rossio,
Joe Stillman, Roger S.H. Schulman
Producers: Jeffrey Katzenberg,
Aron Warner, John H. Williams
Co-producers: Ted Elliott,
Terry Rossio
Associate producer: Jane Hartwell
Executive producers: Penney
Finkelman Cox, Sandra Rabins,
Steven Spielberg (uncredited)
Cast: Mike Myers (voice),
Eddie Murphy (voice), Cameron
Diaz (voice)
Opened May 18, 2001

Evolution
(Columbia/DreamWorks/Montecito)
Director: Ivan Reitman
Screenplay: David Diamond, David
Weissman, Don Jakoby
Producers: Daniel Goldberg, Joe
Medjuck, Ivan Reitman
Co-producer: Paul Deason
Associate producers: Sheldon Kahn,
Ken Schwenker, Ronell Venter
Executive producers: Jeff Apple,
Tom Pollock, David Rodgers, Steven
Spielberg (uncredited)
Cast: David Duchovny, Julianne
Moore, Orlando Jones
Opened June 8, 2001

A.I.: Artificial Intelligence
Producers: Bonnie Curtis, Kathleen
Kennedy, Steven Spielberg
Executive producers: Jan Harlan,
Walter Parkes

Jurassic Park III
(Universal/Amblin)
Director: Joe Johnston
Screenplay: Peter Buchman,
Alexander Payne, Jim Taylor
Producers: Larry J. Franco,
Kathleen Kennedy
Associate producers: Cheryl A. Tkach,
David Womark
Executive producer: Steven Spielberg
Cast: Sam Neill, William H. Macy,
Téa Leoni
Opened July 18, 2001

Men in Black II
(Columbia/Amblin/
MacDonald-Parkes)
Director: Barry Sonnenfeld
Screenplay: Robert Gordon,
Barry Fanaro
Producers: Laurie MacDonald,
Walter Parkes
Co-producer: Graham Place
Associate producers: Marc Haimes,
Stephanie Kemp
Executive producer: Steven Spielberg
Cast: Tommy Lee Jones, Will Smith,
Rip Torn
Opened July 3, 2002

Catch Me If You Can
Producers: Walter Parkes,
Steven Spielberg
Co-producer: Devorah Moos-Hankin
Associate producer: Sergio
Mimica-Gezzan
Executive producers: Barry Kemp,
Laurie MacDonald, Tony Romano,
Michel Shane
Co-executive producer: Daniel Lupi

The Terminal
Producers: Laurie MacDonald,
Walter Parkes, Steven Spielberg
Co-producer: Sergio Mimica-Gezzan
Executive producers: Jason Hoffs,
Andrew Niccol, Patricia Whitcher

The Legend of Zorro
(Columbia/Amblin/
Tornado/Spyglass)
Director: Martin Campbell
Screenplay: Roberto Orci,
Alex Kurtzman
Producers: Laurie MacDonald, Walter
Parkes, Lloyd Phillips
Co-producers: John Gertz, Marc
Haimes, Amy Reid Lescoe
Executive producers: Gary Barber,
Roger Birnbaum, Steven Spielberg
Cast: Antonio Banderas,
Catherine Zeta-Jones, Rufus Sewell
Opened October 28, 2005

Memoirs of a Geisha
(Columbia/DreamWorks/Spyglass/
Amblin/Red Wagon)
Director: Rob Marshall
Screenplay: Robin Swicord
Producers: Lucy Fisher, Steven
Spielberg, Douglas Wick
Co-producer: John DeLuca
Executive producers: Gary Barber,
Roger Birnbaum, Bobby Cohen,
Patricia Whitcher
Cast: Ziyi Zhang, Ken Watanabe,
Michelle Yeoh
Opened December 23, 2005

Munich
Producers: Kathleen Kennedy,
Barry Mendel, Steven Spielberg,
Colin Wilson
Assistant producer: Vincent Servant

Monster House
(Columbia/Relativity/ImageMovers/
Amblin/Sony Animation)
Director: Gil Kenan
Screenplay: Dan Harmon, Rob
Schrab, Pamela Pettler
Producers: Jack Rapke, Steve Starkey
Associate producers: Heather Smith
Kelton, Bennett Schneir
Executive producers: Jason Clark,
Steven Spielberg, Robert Zemeckis
Line producer: Peter M. Tobyansen
Cast: Mitchel Musso (voice), Sam
Lerner (voice), Spencer Locke (voice)
Opened July 21, 2006

Flags of Our Fathers
(DreamWorks/Warner Bros./
Amblin/Malpaso)
Director: Clint Eastwood
Screenplay: William Broyles Jr.,
Paul Haggis
Producers: Clint Eastwood,
Robert Lorenz, Steven Spielberg
Co-producer: Tim Moore
Cast: Ryan Phillippe, Jesse Bradford,
Adam Beach
Opened October 20, 2006

Letters from Iwo Jima
(DreamWorks/Warner Bros./
Amblin/Malpaso)
Director: Clint Eastwood
Screenplay: Iris Yamashita
Producers: Clint Eastwood,
Robert Lorenz, Steven Spielberg
Co-producer: Tim Moore
Executive producer: Paul Haggis
Cast: Ken Watanabe, Kazunari
Ninomiya, Tsuyoshi Ihara
Opened February 2, 2007

Transformers
(DreamWorks/Paramount/
Hasbro/Di Bonaventura/
SprocketHeads/thinkfilm)
Director: Michael Bay
Screenplay: Alex Kurtzman,
Roberto Orci
Producers: Ian Bryce, Tom
DeSanto, Lorenzo di Bonaventura,
Don Murphy
Co-producers: Ken Bates,
Allegra Clegg
Associate producers: Matthew
Cohan, Michelle McGonagle
Executive producers: Michael Bay,
Brian Goldner, Steven Spielberg,
Mark Vahradian
Cast: Shia LaBeouf, Megan Fox,
Josh Duhamel
Opened July 3, 2007

Eagle Eye
(DreamWorks/Goldcrest/KMP)
Director: D.J. Caruso
Screenplay: John Glenn, Travis
Adam Wright, Hillary Seitz,
Dan McDermott
Producers: Patrick Crowley, Alex
Kurtzman, Roberto Orci
Co-producer: Pete Chiarelli
Associate producers: James
M. Freitag, Rizelle Mendoza
Executive producers: Edward L.
McDonnell, Steven Spielberg
Cast: Shia LaBeouf, Michelle
Monaghan, Rosario Dawson,
Michael Chiklis
Opened September 26, 2008

**Transformers:
Revenge of the Fallen**
(DreamWorks/Paramount/Hasbro/
Di Bonaventura)
Director: Michael Bay
Screenplay: Ehren Kruger, Alex
Kurtzman, Roberto Orci
Producers: Ian Bryce, Tom DeSanto,
Lorenzo di Bonaventura, Don Murphy
Co-producers: Ken Bates,
Allegra Clegg
Associate producers: Matthew Cohan,
K.C. Hodenfield, Michelle McGonagle
Executive producers: Michael Bay,
Brian Goldner, Steven Spielberg,
Mark Vahradian
Cast: Shia LaBeouf, Megan Fox,
Josh Duhamel
Opened June 24, 2009

The Lovely Bones
(DreamWorks/Film4/
WingNut/New Zealand Large
Budget Screen Production Grant/
Goldcrest [uncredited]/
Key Creatives [uncredited])
Director: Peter Jackson
Screenplay: Fran Walsh, Philippa
Boyens, Peter Jackson
Producers: Carolynne Cunningham,
Peter Jackson, Aimee Peyronnet,
Fran Walsh
Co-producers: Marc Ashton, Philippa
Boyens, Anne Bruning
Executive producers: Ken Kamins,
Tessa Ross, Steven Spielberg,
James Wilson
Cast: Rachel Weisz, Mark Wahlberg,
Saoirse Ronan
Opened January 15, 2010

Hereafter
(Warner Bros./Kennedy-Marshall/
Malpaso/Amblin)
Director: Clint Eastwood
Screenplay: Peter Morgan
Producers: Clint Eastwood, Kathleen
Kennedy, Robert Lorenz
Executive producers: Frank
Marshall, Tim Moore, Peter Morgan,
Steven Spielberg
Line producer (France):
John Bernard
Cast: Matt Damon, Cécile De France,
Bryce Dallas Howard
Opened October 22, 2010

True Grit
(Paramount/Skydance/Scott Rudin/
Mike Zoss)
Directors: Ethan Coen, Joel Coen
Screenplay: Ethan Coen, Joel Coen
Producers: Ethan Coen, Joel Coen,
Scott Rudin
Executive producers: David Ellison,
Megan Ellison, Robert Graf, Paul
Schwake, Steven Spielberg
Cast: Jeff Bridges, Hailee Steinfeld,
Matt Damon, Josh Brolin
Opened December 22, 2010

Super 8
(Paramount/Amblin/Bad Robot)
Director: J.J. Abrams
Screenplay: J.J. Abrams
Producers: J.J. Abrams, Bryan Burk,
Steven Spielberg
Associate producers: Udi Nedivi,
Michelle Rejwan, Ben Rosenblatt
Executive producer: Guy Riedel
Cast: Elle Fanning, Amanda Michalka,
Kyle Chandler
Opened June 10, 2011

Transformers: Dark of the Moon
(Paramount/Hasbro/
Di Bonaventura)
Director: Michael Bay
Screenplay: Ehren Kruger
Producers: Ian Bryce, Tom DeSanto,
Lorenzo di Bonaventura, Don Murphy
Co-producers: Ken Bates,
Allegra Clegg
Associate producers: Matthew Cohan,
Michael Kase, Linda Pianigiani
Executive producers: Michael Bay,
Brian Goldner, Steven Spielberg,
Mark Vahradian
3D producer: Michelle McGonagle
Cast: Shia LaBeouf, Rosie
Huntington-Whiteley, Tyrese Gibson
Opened June 28, 2011

Cowboys & Aliens
(Universal/DreamWorks/
Reliance/Relativity/Imagine/
K/O/Fairview/Platinum)
Director: Jon Favreau
Screenplay: Roberto Orci, Alex
Kurtzman, Damon Lindelof, Mark
Fergus, Hawk Ostby
Producers: Johnny Dodge, Brian
Grazer, Ron Howard, Alex Kurtzman,
Damon Lindelof, Roberto Orci, Scott
Mitchell Rosenberg
Co-producers: Daniel Forcey,
Karen Gilchrist, K.C. Hodenfield,
Chris Wade
Executive producers: Bobby Cohen,
Jon Favreau, Randy Greenberg,
Ryan Kavanaugh, Steven Spielberg,
Denis L. Stewart
Cast: Daniel Craig, Harrison Ford,
Olivia Wilde
Opened July 29, 2011

Real Steel
(Touchstone/DreamWorks/21 Laps/
Angry/ImageMovers/Reliance)
Director: Shawn Levy
Screenplay: John Gatins
Producers: Shawn Levy,
Susan Montford, Don Murphy,
Robert Zemeckis
Co-producers: Rick Benattar,
Eric Hedayat
Executive producers: Josh McLaglen,
Mary McLaglen, Jack Rapke, Steven
Spielberg, Steve Starkey
Cast: Hugh Jackman, Evangeline
Lilly, Dakota Goyo
Opened October 7, 2011

**The Adventures of Tintin:
The Secret of the Unicorn**
Producers: Peter Jackson, Kathleen
Kennedy, Steven Spielberg
Co-producer: Jason D. McGatlin
Associate producer: Adam Somner
Executive producers: Ken Kamins,
Nick Rodwell, Stephane Sperry

War Horse
Producers: Kathleen Kennedy,
Steven Spielberg
Co-producers: Tracey Seaward,
Adam Somner
Executive producers: Revel Guest,
Frank Marshall

Men in Black III
(Amblin/Media Magik/
Parkes-MacDonald)
Director: Barry Sonnenfeld
Screenplay: Etan Cohen,
David Koepp, Jeff Nathanson,
Michael Soccio
Producers: Laurie MacDonald,
Walter Parkes
Executive producers: G. Mac Brown,
Steven Spielberg
Cast: Will Smith, Tommy Lee Jones,
Josh Brolin
Opened May 25, 2012

Lincoln
Producers: Kathleen Kennedy,
Steven Spielberg
Co-producer: Adam Somner
Executive producer: Daniel Lupi

Other productions

Amazing Stories
(Amblin/Universal Television)
TV series, 1985–1987
Executive producer (45 episodes)

Tummy Trouble
(Amblin/Walt Disney)
Short, 1989
Executive producer

**Warner Bros. Celebration of
Tradition, June 2, 1990**
(Warner Bros.)
TV documentary, 1990
Executive producer

Roller Coaster Rabbit
(Amblin/Touchstone)
Short, 1990
Executive producer

Back to the Future
(Amblin/Universal Cartoon Studios)
TV series, 1991
Executive producer (1 episode)

A Brief History of Time
(Amblin/Anglia/Channel Four)
Documentary, 1991
Executive producer (uncredited)

A Wish for Wings That Work
(Amblin/Universal Cartoon Studios/
Universal Television)
TV short, 1991
Executive producer (uncredited)

**Tiny Toon Adventures:
How I Spent My Vacation**
(Amblin/Warner Bros. Animation)
Video, 1992
Executive producer

The Plucky Duck Show
(Amblin/Warner Bros. Animation)
TV series, 1992
Executive producer

Fievel's American Tails
(Amblin/Universal Cartoon
Studios/Nelvana)
TV series, 1992
Executive producer (13 episodes)

Tiny Toon Adventures
(Amblin/Warner Bros. Animation)
TV series, 1990–1992
Executive producer (98 episodes)

Trail Mix-Up
(Amblin/Walt Disney)
Short, 1993
Executive producer

Class of '61
(Amblin/Universal Television)
TV movie, 1993
Executive producer

Family Dog
(Amblin/Universal Television)
TV series, 1993
Executive producer (1 episode)

SeaQuest DSV
(Amblin/Universal Television)
TV series, 1993–1995
Executive producer (44 episodes)

Animaniacs
(Amblin/Warner Bros. Animation)
TV series, 1993–1998
Executive producer (93 episodes)

**Yakko's World: An Animaniacs
Singalong**
(Amblin/Warner Bros. Animation)
Video, 1994
Executive producer

Tiny Toons Spring Break
(Amblin/Warner Bros. Animation)
TV movie, 1994
Executive producer

I'm Mad
(Amblin/Warner Bros.)
Short, 1994
Executive producer

Pinky & the Brain
(Amblin/Warner Bros. Animation)
TV series, 1995–1998
Executive producer (70 episodes)

**A Pinky & the Brain
Christmas Special**
(Amblin/Warner Bros. Animation)
TV movie, 1995
Executive producer

Tiny Toons' Night Ghoulery
(Amblin/Warner Bros. Animation)
TV movie, 1995
Executive producer

Survivors of the Holocaust
(Survivors of the Shoah Visual History
Foundation/Turner)
TV documentary, 1996
Executive producer

High Incident
(ABC/Donwell/DreamWorks)
TV series, 1996–1997
Executive producer (2 episodes)

The Best of Roger Rabbit
(Amblin/Walt Disney)
Video, 1996
Executive producer

The Lost Children of Berlin
(Survivors of the Shoah Visual History
Foundation/Fogwood)
Documentary, 1997
Executive producer

Freakazoid!
(Amblin/Warner Bros. Animation)
TV series, 1997
Executive producer (1 episode)

Toonsylvania
(DreamWorks)
TV series, 1998
Executive producer (1 episode)

The Last Days
(Survivors of the Shoah Visual
History Foundation/Ken Lipper-
June Beallor)
Documentary, 1998
Executive producer

Pinky, Elmyra & the Brain
(Amblin/Warner Bros. Animation)
TV series, 1998–1999
Executive producer (9 episodes)

Wakko's Wish
(Amblin/TMS/
Warner Bros. Animation)
Video, 1999
Executive producer (uncredited)

Eyes of the Holocaust
(Survivors of the Shoah Visual History
Foundation/InterCom)
Documentary, 2000
Executive producer

Shooting War
(DreamWorks/Lorac)
TV documentary, 2000
Executive producer

Semper Fi
(DreamWorks/NBC/Peculiar)
TV movie, 2001
Executive producer

Band of Brothers
(DreamWorks/HBO/Playtone/BBC)
TV mini-series, 2001
Executive producer (2 episodes)

We Stand Alone Together
(Cowen-Richter/DreamWorks/
HBO/Playtone)
TV documentary, 2001
Executive producer

Broken Silence
(Survivors of the Shoah
Visual History Foundation/
Cinemax Reel Life/Historias
Cinematográficas Cinemania)
TV mini-series documentary, 2002
Executive producer

Price for Peace
(National D-Day Museum)
Documentary, 2002
Executive producer

Taken
(DreamWorks)
TV mini-series, 2002
Executive producer (1 episode)

Burma Bridge Busters
(National D-Day Museum)
TV documentary, 2003
Executive producer

Voices from the List
(Survivors of the Shoah Visual History
Foundation/Allentown)
Video documentary, 2004
Executive producer

**Dan Finnerty & the Dan Band:
I Am Woman**
(Coming Home/DreamWorks)
TV movie, 2005
Executive producer

Into the West
(DreamWorks/Voice)
TV mini-series, 2005
Executive producer

Spell Your Name
(USC Shoah Foundation Institute/
Film Plus)
Documentary, 2006
Executive producer

The Big Bad Heist
(DreamWorks/IMAGEN/
Mark Burnett)
Short, 2007
Executive producer

Dance with the Devil
(DreamWorks/IMAGEN/
Mark Burnett)
Short, 2007
Executive producer

On the Lot
(Amblin/DreamWorks/
Mark Burnett)
TV series, 2007
Executive producer (4 episodes)

United States of Tara
(DreamWorks)
TV series, 2009–2011
Executive producer (36 episodes)

The Pacific
(DreamWorks/HBO/Playtone)
TV mini-series, 2010
Executive producer (10 episodes)

Rising: Rebuilding Ground Zero
(DreamWorks/KPI)
TV series documentary, 2011
Executive producer

Falling Skies
(DreamWorks/Invasion)
TV series, 2011
Executive producer (10 episodes)

Terra Nova
(Amblin/Chernin/Kapital/Siesta/
Twentieth Century Fox)
TV series, 2011
Executive producer (10 episodes)

Locke & Key
(Amblin/Davis/DreamWorks)
TV movie, 2011
Executive producer

The River
(ABC/DreamWorks)
TV series, 2011
Executive producer (1 episode)

Transformers: The Ride (3D)
(Universal Creative)
Backdrop to theme-park ride, 2011
Executive producer

Smash
(DreamWorks/Storyline/UMS)
TV series, 2012
Executive producer (14 episodes)

The Talisman
(Amblin/DreamWorks/
Kennedy-Marshall)
TV mini-series, 2012
Executive producer

Spielberg with the two most important women in his life, his mother Leah and his wife Kate Capshaw, celebrating the two Oscars for *Schindler's List* in 1994.

Picture credits

The majority of the photographs in this book have been sourced through the Steven Spielberg Archive. Every effort has been made to trace and acknowledge the copyright holders. We apologize in advance for any unintentional omissions and would be pleased, if any such case should arise, to add appropriate acknowledgment in any future edition of the book.

T: top; B: bottom; R: right; L: left; C: center; BG: background

The Steven Spielberg Archive: 1, 6 (Sony), 10–19, 20–21 (Universal), 24 (Paramount), 27 (Universal), 28 (Universal), 32 (Universal), 34–41 (Universal), 44–45 (Universal), 46 TL, TR (Universal), 49 (Universal), 50 TR, BR (Universal), 51 L (Universal), 56 B (Sony), 57 L (Sony), 58 BR (Sony), 59 BL (Sony), 61 (Sony), 63 B (Sony), 64 TL, TR, B ROW (Sony), 68 L, TR (Sony), 70–71 (Universal), 73 (Universal), 76 B (Paramount), 77 (Paramount), 86 T (Universal), 88 T, B (Universal), 88–89 (Universal), 89 T (Universal), 90 L (Universal), 106 L (Warner Bros.), 108 (Warner Bros.), 110 TL, B (Warner Bros.), 111 TL, TR (Warner Bros.), 115 T (Warner Bros.), 123 (Paramount), 125 B (Paramount), 138 B (Sony), 140 TL, CL, BL (Sony), 146–147 (Universal), 151 TL, TR, C, BL (Universal), 152 (Sony), 154 (Universal), 156 TL (Universal), 159 T (Universal), 162 L (Universal), 166 R (Universal), 168–169, 171 R (Universal), 178–179 (Paramount), 182–183 (Paramount), 184 T3 (Paramount), 186 B (Paramount), 189 L (Paramount), 190 (Paramount), 195 TR (Warner Bros.), 198 L (Warner Bros.), 199 R (Warner Bros.), 202 T (Fox), 204 B (Fox), 210 (Paramount), 213 (Paramount), 214 B ROW (Paramount), 215 T (Paramount), 216 (Paramount), 218 T, B (Paramount), 220 (Paramount), 222 B (Paramount), 226 TL (Paramount), 228–229 (Paramount), 231 (Paramount), 234 TL, TR, BR (Universal), 236 L (Universal), 237 L, R (Universal), 251 B (Paramount), 252 (Paramount), 265 (Bruce McBroom MPTV), 280 (National Museum of American Jewish History); **David James:** 2, 269; **Corbis:** 5 (Mitchell Gerber), 9 (Eric Ogden), 72 R (Sunset Boulevard), 84 (Sunset Boulevard), 156 TR (Peter Turnley), 250 L (Stéphane Cardinale / People Avenue), 264 (John Russo), 277 (Steve Starr), 279 (Sunset Boulevard); **Universal:** 23, 30 L, 46 BR, 47, 49 BR, 53 T, B, 67, 72 L, 86 B, 92 B, 131, 135, 145, 150, 156 B, 158, 159 B, 162 R, 165, 167, 170, 233, 236 R, 238; **Alamy:** 29 T, B (Universal), 51 TR (Universal), 65 (Sony), 68 BR, 88 C (Universal), 93 (Universal), 132 B (Universal), 139 R (Sony), 142 R (Sony), 148 (Universal), 151 BC, BR (Universal), 160 (Universal), 163 (Universal), 166 L (Universal), 184 ABOVE B, 186 T (Paramount), 195 TL (Warner Bros.), 197 T (Warner Bros.), 202 B (Fox), 203, 212, 214 T (Paramount), 215 B (Paramount), 251 TR (Paramount); **Kobal:** 29 C (Universal), 33 (Universal), 43 (Universal), 46 BL (Universal), 48 (Universal), 50 L, 51 BR (Universal), 52 (Universal), 58 T (Columbia/Sony), 60 T (Sony), 62 T (Sony), 64 C (Sony), 68 BL (Universal), 79 BC (Lucasfilm/Paramount), 80–81 (Paramount), 82 TL, BR (Paramount), 87 T (Universal), 91 (Universal), 92 T (Universal), 96 B (Paramount), 98 T (Paramount), 101 (Paramount), 109 TR (Warner Bros.), 113 (Warner Bros.), 126 L (Lucasfilm/Paramount), 132 T (Universal), 133 L, R (Universal), 134 L (Universal), 137 (Sony), 142 L (Sony), 149 TR, BR (Universal), 180 (Paramount), 185 (Paramount), 187 T (Paramount), 188 T (Paramount), 201 (Fox), 204 CR (Fox), 205 TR, B (Fox), 206–207 (Fox), 208 (DreamWorks/Paramount), 221 T, B (DreamWorks/Paramount), 222 T (DreamWorks/Paramount), 223 (DreamWorks/Paramount), 235 R (Universal), 249 (Paramount); **www.cinemaposter.com:** 30 TR (Universal); **Archivesdu7eArt/DR:** 30 BR (Universal), 31 (Universal), 246 BG (Paramount); **Sony:** 55, 56 T, 57 R, 58 BL, 59 BR, 60 B, 62 B, 63 T, 138 T, 141; **Everett Collection:** 69 T (Universal), 79 B (Paramount); **Lucasfilm Image Archive:** 75 (Paramount), 76 T (Paramount), 78 (Paramount), 79 T, TC (Paramount), 82 TR, BL (Paramount), 83 L, R (Paramount), 94 (Paramount), 96 TL, TR (Paramount), 97 (Paramount), 98 B (Paramount), 99 (Paramount), 100 T, B (Paramount), 102–103 (Paramount), 124 L, R (Paramount), 125 TL, TR (Paramount), 127 (Paramount), 128–129 (Paramount), 198 R (Warner Bros.), 204 T, CL (Fox), 230 (Paramount), 241 (Paramount), 242–245 (Paramount), 246 B (Paramount), 247 (Paramount); **Warner Bros.:** 105, 107, 109 TL, B, 110 TR, 114, 116 TL, TR, BL, BR, 117 TR, TL, BR, 118–119, 120, 121 T, B, 193, 194 B, 197 B; **Album:** 143 R (Sony); **Paramount:** 173–177, 184 BL, 189 R, 219, 225, 226 B, 227 T, 251 TL; **WETA Digital:** 253 TL, TC, TR, BL, BR (Paramount), 253 C (Paramount/Everett Collection), 254 T, B (Paramount), 255 T (Paramount/Everett Collection), 270 (Chris Guise); **DreamWorks:** 256 (Andrew Cooper), 258, 259 T (Andrew Cooper), 259 B, 260 TL (David Abbleby), 260 TR (Andrew Cooper), 260 B, 261 B (Andrew Cooper), 261 (David Abbleby), 263, 266; **WireImage:** 262 L (Eric Charbonneau).

All DreamWorks stills: Courtesy of DreamWorks II Distribution Co., LLC, all rights reserved. All Sony stills, all rights reserved, including: *Close Encounters of the Third Kind* © 1977 renewed 2005 Columbia Pictures Industries, Inc. Courtesy of Columbia Pictures; *Hook* © 1991 Tristar Pictures, Inc. Courtesy of Tristar Pictures. All Paramount film stills © Paramount Pictures Corporation, all rights reserved, including: *Amistad* © DW Studios LLC; *Catch Me If You Can* © DW Studios LLC; *Raiders of the Lost Ark* © Lucasfilm Ltd. (LFL) 1981; *Indiana Jones and the Last Crusade* © Lucasfilm Ltd. (LFL) 1989; *Indiana Jones and the Temple of Doom* © Lucasfilm Ltd. (LFL) 1984; *Indiana Jones and the Kingdom of the Crystal Skull* © Lucasfilm Ltd. (LFL) 2008; *Saving Private Ryan* © DW Studios LLC and Paramount Pictures and Amblin Entertainment; *The Terminal* © DW Studios LLC; *The Adventures of Tintin* © DW Studios LLC and Columbia Pictures Industries, Inc; *War of the Worlds* © 2005 by DW Studios LLC and Paramount Pictures. All Universal film stills: Courtesy of Universal Studios Licensing LLLP, all rights reserved (*E.T.* photography by Bruce McBroom). All Warner Bros. film stills: Licensed by Warner Bros. Entertainment Inc, all rights reserved.

Sources

With the exception of the sources listed below, all quotes by Steven Spielberg are taken from interviews with Richard Schickel.

Page 1 In *Masters of Cinema: Steven Spielberg* by Clelia Cohen, *Cahiers du Cinéma*, 2010, p.7; 12, 22, 248 Interview with Ruben V. Nepales, *What Excites Steven Spielberg?*, http://entertainment.inquirer.net; 14, 28, 48, 83, 182, 184, 280 Interview with James Lipton on *Inside the Actor's Studio*, 1999; 18, 66, 99, 114, 163, 254 Interview with Anthony Breznican, *Entertainment Weekly*, 2011; 25, 74, 79, 157, 178, 196, 239, 246 Interview with Jim Windolf, *Vanity Fair*, 2008; 15, 26, 40, 122, 130, 153, 188 In *The Complete Spielberg* by Ian Freer, Virgin, 2001, p.26, ibid, p.44, p.171, p.191, p.220, p.273; 35 Interview with Mitch Tuchman in *Film Comment* (1978), in *Steven Spielberg Interviews* by Lester D. Friedman and Brent Notbohm (eds.), University Press Mississippi, 2000, p.47; 38 Interview with David Helpern in *Take One* (1974), in *Steven Spielberg Interviews* by Friedman and Notbohm (eds.), p.6; 41, 47, 53, 61, 95, 126 In *Spielberg: Father of the Man* by Andrew Yule, Little, Brown, 1996, p.47, p.68, p.76, p.106, p.238, p.300; 42, 44 In *Nigel Andrews on Jaws* by Nigel Andrews, Bloomsbury, 1999, p.32, p.32; 54 Interview with Richard Combs in *Sight & Sound* (1977), in *Steven Spielberg Interviews* by Friedman and Notbohm (eds.), p.31; 63 From the Directors Guild of America, *A Tribute to Steven Spielberg*, 2011; 85 Interview with Michael Sragow in *Rolling Stone* (1982), in *Steven Spielberg Interviews* by Friedman and Notbohm (eds.), p.117; 89, 224 Interview with Mark Lawson for BBC Radio 4's *Front Row*, 2012; 91 In *Blockbuster—How Hollywood Learned to Stop Worrying and Love the Summer* by Tom Shone, Simon & Schuster, 2004, p.136; 104 Interview with Glenn Collins in *New York Times* (1985), in *Steven Spielberg Interviews* by Friedman and Notbohm (eds.), p.122; 112, 136, 265 In *The Films of Steven Spielberg* by Douglas Brode, Citadel Press, 1995, p.143, p.204, p.11; 116, 119 Interview with Myra Forsberg in *New York Times* (1988), in *Steven Spielberg Interviews* by Friedman and Notbohm (eds.), p.129, ibid; 140 Interview with Ana Maria Bahiana in *Cinema Papers* (1992), in *Steven Spielberg Interviews* by Friedman and Notbohm (eds.), p.154; 144 Interview with Stephen Schiff in *New Yorker* (1994), in *Steven Spielberg Interviews* by Friedman and Notbohm (eds.), p.176; 149 From "The Spielberg Formula," *Harper's Magazine*, 1998, p.32; 155, 160 From "The Real Thing" by Zoe Heller, *Independent on Sunday*, 1993, p.27, p.24; 164, 169 Interview with Peter Biskind in *Premiere* (1997), in *Steven Spielberg Interviews* by Friedman and Notbohm (eds.), p.198, pp.200–201; 167 From "The Man With a Monster Talent" by Ian Johnstone, *Sunday Times*, 1997, p.12; 172, 200 From "Inside the Dream Factory" by Stephen J. Dubner, *Observer Magazine*, 1999, p.15, p.18; 191 Interview with Stephen Pizzello in *American Cinematographer* (1998), in *Steven Spielberg Interviews* by Friedman and Notbohm (eds.), p.208; 204 Interview with Alec Cawthorne, www.bbc.co.uk/films; 209, 212 Interview with Steve Head, http://uk.movies.ign.com; 217, 220 Interview with Jenny Cooney, *Total Film*, 2004; 228 Interview with Dan Portnoy, www.thecinemasource.com; 240 Interview on www.examiner.com; 247 Interview with Terrence Rafferty, *Creator of the Lost Art*, www.scotsman.com; 257 Interview *War Horse Brought Spielberg to Tears* on www.canada.com/entertainment; 258 Interview on www.moviesonline.ca; 268 Interview *What I've Learnt: Steven Spielberg* on www.timeslive.co.za/lifestyle.

Acknowledgments

Palazzo Editions would like to thank the following for their help and contribution to this book. At DreamWorks, Kathleen Kennedy, Marvin Levy, Kristie Macosko, Kristin Stark, Mary Hulett, and Sam Becker. At the Steven Spielberg Archive, Michelle Fandetti, Meghan Foreman, and Lisa Matz. At Palazzo Editorial, Stephanie Bramwell-Lawes, Matthew Coniam, James Hodgson, Matthew Perry, and Chloe Pew Latter; at Palazzo Design, Ben Hamilton and Rob Payne (at Mark Thomson Studio). At XY Digital, Eric Bailey Ladd, Terry Jeavons, and Dave King. At Imago Publishing, Andy Hannan. For their help with the images: Dave Kent and Phil Moad at the Kobal Collection; Adele Hayes at Alamy; Nye Jones and Toby Hopkins at Corbis; Philip Grimwood Jones at Getty. At Universal, Roni Lubliner, Deidre Thieman, Jamie A. Braucht. At Sony (SPE Archives & Collections), Colin Greene and Gilbert Emralino. At Paramount Pictures, Flora Lopez, Larry McCallister, and Andrea Kalas. At LucasFilm Image Archives, Tina Mills. At Warner Brothers Entertainment, Julie S. Heath. At Walt Disney Studios, Steve Newman.

Opposite: On the set of *Close Encounters of the Third Kind*, 1977.

Overleaf: Spielberg's very first experiments in film as a teenager were made using this handheld 8mm camera.

"Every movie is really a time capsule, when you finish a film and you say goodbye to your cast and crew you've buried a piece of your life right there on that set, you know, and that's going to stay there forever."